WITHDRAWN

School Songs of
America's Colleges
and
Universities

SCHOOL SONGS OF AMERICA'S COLLEGES AND UNIVERSITIES

A DIRECTORY

COMPILED AND
EDITED BY

Robert F. O'Brien

Greenwood Press
NEW YORK · WESTPORT, CONNECTICUT · LONDON

Library of Congress Cataloging-in-Publication Data

O'Brien, Robert F.
    School songs of America's colleges and universities : a directory
/ compiled and edited by Robert F. O'Brien.
      p. cm.
    Includes bibliographical references and indexes.
    ISBN 0-313-27890-3 (alk. paper)
    1. Students' songs—United States—Bibliography. 2. Universities
and colleges—United States—Songs and music—Bibliography.
I. Title.
    ML128.S7502   1991
    782.42'159—dc20   91-11337

British Library Cataloguing in Publication Data is available.

Library of Congress Catalog Card Number: 91-11337
ISBN: 0-313-27890-3

First published in 1991

Greenwood Press, 88 Post Road West, Westport, CT 06881
An imprint of Greenwood Publishing Group, Inc.

Printed in the United States of America

The paper used in this book complies with the
Permanent Paper Standard issued by the National
Information Standards Organization (Z39.48-1984).

10 9 8 7 6 5 4 3 2 1

Contents

Abbreviations

am   alma mater

fs   fight song

m   music

ma   music adapted

o   other song

oam   arranged by other alma mater

ofs   other fight song

p/c   publisher copyright

PD   public domain

w   words

wa   words adapted

Preface

Directors of performing organizations are frequently called upon to provide appropriate music for honored guests, lecturers, and public figures throughout the academic year as well as at concerts, athletic events, social events, and graduation ceremonies. Many times it is appropriate to perform school songs with which the guests or organizations are associated. Alumni and friends also ask for sources of fight songs, alma maters, and other school songs to obtain music for performers at weddings, alumni gatherings, and fraternal meetings as well as for occasions such as funerals and ritual ceremonies.

During my thirty-three-year tenure as Director of Bands and music arranger for the University of Notre Dame I often wished I had had a reference source of school songs to assist me in locating titles, composers, and publisher sources. Since it is imperative for arrangers to seek copyright and performance permissions and to give credit to composers and arrangers whenever possible, it is hoped that this directory will save many hours of time-consuming research.

The directory serves as a permanent record of the school songs of America's colleges and universities. I thank the many schools that responded to national mailings and made this reference possible. The basis for my selection of the schools which are represented in the directory is predicated on the response I received from the institutions that answered questionnaires which were sent in the course of four national mailings. The schools contacted were those listed in Lovejoy's College Guide. Information about some non-responding schools was taken from material found in the music credit file used by the University of Notre Dame Band office and from general library sources.

Some of the institutions listed have changed their names, merged with other schools or are no longer operational. The songs of these colleges are recorded for historical reasons and, in some cases, for the sentimental interest of the alumni of these schools.

This directory has been made possible in no small part by the suggestions and cooperation of many people and organizations. I am particularly thankful to Catherine O'Brien and Dr. James Johnson for their suggestions and encouragement. I am grateful for the assistance of Richard Conklin of the University of Notre Dame Public Information Office and John Heisler of the University of Notre Dame Sports Information Office. Finally, I thank my friends and colleagues of the University of Notre Dame Band: Dr. Luther Snavely, Director of Bands; Prof. James Phillips, Associate Director of Bands; and Rev. George Wiskirchen, Assistant Director of Bands, whose multiple duties include script writing and music credit preparation.

Introduction: The School Song

When you hear a fight song or an alma mater, you are hearing the hopes and aspirations of generations of young people; you are sharing in their determination to "win over all"; you are feeling their love for their alma maters; and you are caught up in their excitement and steadfast support of their team and their school. Only a school song can unite all students, past and present, in a continuity that is truly inspiring.

The fight song has always been with us in one form or another and is possibly of military origin. Today, it is the rallying call for teams in athletic combat. The fight song is an inspiration for students and their teams as it unites the campus in a common cause.

Many of the most enduring fight songs and alma maters were written or adapted in the late 1800s and early 1900s from religious hymns, folk tunes or patriotic songs. However, composers and lyricists are still being inspired by their schools and continue to provide a steady stream of great songs to add to the college legend.

Our school songs are melodies and words that never grow old. The young have sung them for at least 100 years, and the young will continue to do so for generations to come. When people say, "They're singing our song!" it could well be their fight song or their alma mater.

This directory is organized alphabetically by state and, within the state, alphabetically by the name of the institution. Each entry provides the name of the alma mater, fight song, or other major songs associated with the school. Wherever possible, information is provided on the composer, the tune, and publisher or copyright status. Access to the information is augmented through lists of school names, song sources, and references. A list of publishers provides addresses where scores can be secured. A lengthy index of school songs listed alphabetically by title completes the work.

School Songs of
America's Colleges
and
Universities

ALABAMA

ALABAMA A & M UNIVERSITY, Normal

The University Hymn (am) by J. F. Drake (w), no (m) credit given, arr. Henry Bradford, Jr., p/c not listed

Stand Up and Cheer (fs) (Tune, I'm a Jayhawk [University of Kansas], refer to Song Sources)

The Alumni Hymn (o) by Thomas M. Elmore (w) (Tune, Ewing), arr. Henry Bradford, Jr., p/c not listed

ALABAMA STATE UNIVERSITY, Montgomery

Alma Mater (am) (Tune, America the Beautiful, refer to Song Sources)

Fight Song (fs) by Thomas Lyle, p/c not listed

AUBURN UNIVERSITY, Auburn

Auburn Alma Mater (am) by William T. Wood, p/c Thornton W. Allen (c) [1936]

War Eagle (fs) by Al Stillman (w) and Robert Allen (m), p/c Auburn Alumni Association (c) [1955]

Glory to Ole Auburn (o) (Tune, Battle Hymn of the Republic, refer to Song Sources)

BIRMINGHAM-SOUTHERN COLLEGE, Birmingham

On the City's Western Border (am), no w/m credit given, p/c not listed

JACKSONVILLE STATE UNIVERSITY, Jacksonville

Alma Mater (am) by James Rayburn, arr. David L. Walters, p/c not listed

Jax State Fight Song (fs) by David L. Walters, p/c not listed

JUDSON COLLEGE, Marion

Mother Judson (am) by E. L. Powers, p/c Judson College

There'll Always Be a Judson (fs) (Tune, There'll Always Be an England, refer to Song Sources), no (wa) credit given, p/c Judson College

LIVINGSTON UNIVERSITY, Livingston

For the Glory of Old LU (fs) by James Crawford, p/c not listed

Tiger Rag (o) (refer to Song Sources)

MOBILE COLLEGE, Mobile

Mobile College Alma Mater (am) by Wm. Hooper, p/c Mobile College

ST. BERNARD COLLEGE, St. Bernard

Alma Mater (am) by Justin Richard, p/c not listed

Bernardiaus (fs) by Delish and Edwards, p/c not listed

White and Blue (o) (Tune, The Red and Blue [University of Pennsylvania], refer to Song Sources), adapted by Sylvester Faugruan, p/c St. Bernard College

SAMFORD UNIVERSITY, Birmingham

Alma Mater (am), no w/m credit given, p/c not listed

Fight Song (fs), no w/m credit given, p/c not listed

SPRING HILL COLLEGE, Mobile

Purple and White (am) by J. H. Hynes (w) and C. C. Chapman (m), piano arr. Clarence B. Stone and band arr. Chas. Billeaud, p/c Spring Hill College (c) [1931]

STILLMAN COLLEGE, Tuscaloosa

Stillman College Alma Mater (am) (Tune, Annie Lisle, refer to Song Sources)

TALLADEGA COLLEGE, Talladega

Dear Old Talladega (am) by William Picken (w) and E. B. Geer (m), p/c not listed

Walls of Old 'Dega (o) (Tune, Londonderry Air, refer to Song Sources), adapted by Buell G. Gallager, p/c not listed

TROY STATE UNIVERSITY, Troy

Troy State U Alma Mater (am) by Solomon, arr. John Long, p/c not listed

Fight Song (fs) (Tune, Dixie, refer to Song Sources)

Hail to Troy (ofs) by Long, p/c not listed

Trojans, One and All (ofs), no w/m credit given, p/c not listed

TUSKEGEE UNIVERSITY, Tuskegee

The Tuskegee Song (am) by Paul Laurence Dunbar (w) and N. Clark Smith (m), p/c not listed

UNIVERSITY OF ALABAMA, Birmingham

UAB Blazer Fight Song (fs) by Joel Hearn, p/c not listed

UNIVERSITY OF ALABAMA, Tuscaloosa

Alma Mater (am), no w/m credit given, p/c not listed

Yea, Alabama (fs) by Sample, p/c University of Alabama

UNIVERSITY OF MONTEVALLO, Montevallo

Alma Mater (am) by VirginiaPowell Figh (w) and Lucy L. Underwood (m), p/c not listed

UNIVERSITY OF NORTH ALABAMA, Florence

Alma Mater (am), no w/m credit given, p/c not listed

WALKER COLLEGE, Jasper

Walker College Alma Mater (am) by Lou Beville, arr. Everett Lawler, p/c Walker College

Fight Song (fs) (Tune, Dixie, refer to Song Sources), Walker College version arr. Reid Poole, p/c Brodt Music Co.

ALASKA

ALASKA METHODIST UNIVERSITY, Anchorage

Alma Mater (am) by Murray North, p/c Alaska Methodist University

ALASKA PACIFIC UNIVERSITY, Anchorage

Alaska Pacific U. (am) by Donald B. Ward, p/c Donald B. Ward/Alaska Pacific University

SHELDON JACKSON COLLEGE, Sitka

School Song (fs) by J. H. Condit (w) and H. A. Wilkins (m), p/c Sheldon Jackson College

Sheldon Jackson Hymn (o) by Jackson L. Webster (w) and St. Asaph (m), p/c Sheldon Jackson College

UNIVERSITY OF ALASKA, Anchorage

The Seawolves' Song (fs) by Carl Scott and Dan Cox (w) and Carl Scott (m) arr. Carl Scott, p/c C. Scott/D. Cox (c) [1987]

UNIVERSITY OF ALASKA, Fairbanks

University of Alaska Anthem (am) by John Morgan (w) and Dr. John Hopkins (m), p/c John Morgan and Dr. John Hopkins

ARIZONA

ARIZONA STATE UNIVERSITY, Tempe

ASU Alma Mater (am) by Felix E. McKernan, arr. Ed Madden, p/c Arizona State University

Alma Mater (oam) by Ernest Hopkins (w) and Miles Dresskell (m), p/c not listed

Maroon and Gold (fs) by Felix E. McKernan, arr. Ed Madden, p/c Arizona State University

ASU Fight Song (ofs) by Albert O. Davis, p/c not listed

ARIZONA WESTERN COLLEGE, Yuma

Arizona Western College Fight Song (fs) by Harold Hayes, arr. Harold Hayes, p/c not listed (c) [1960]

CENTRAL ARIZONA COLLEGE, Coolidge

All Hail, CAC (am) by Dr. James Hamilton Johnson, p/c Dr. James Hamilton Johnson

Ole! Vaqueros (fs) [Title and words changed to vaqueras and cowgirls for all female athletic events and also to contest when ball game is not appropriate.] by Bill Skinner (w) and Dr. James Hamilton Johnson (m), p/c Dr. James Hamilton Johnson

GLENDALE COMMUNITY COLLEGE, Glendale

Alma Mater (am) by Florine Kitts (w) and Dr. C. Paul Raper (m), p/c Oz Music Publishers

Fight Song (fs) by Dr. Lee Baxter, p/c Oz Music Publishers

NORTHERN ARIZONA UNIVERSITY, Flagstaff

NAU Alma Mater (am), no w/m credit given, arr. D. Wolf, p/c not listed

Fight Song (fs) (Tune, Washington and Lee Swing, refer to Song Sources)

Timber (o) no w/m credit given, arr. D. Wolf, p/c not listed

PHOENIX COLLEGE, Phoenix

Fight PC (fs), no w/m credit given, arr. Albert O. Davis, p/c Phoenix College

UNIVERSITY OF ARIZONA, Tucson

Bear Down Arizona (fs) by Jack Lee, p/c Hal Leonard Publishing Co.

Fight Wild Cats, Fight (ofs) by Doug Holsclaw (w) and Thornton Allen and Doug Holsclaw (m), p/c Thornton W. Allen

All Hail Arizona (o) by Ted Monroe (w) and Dorothy Clayton Monroe (m), p/c not listed

YAVAPAI COLLEGE, Prescott

Rough Riders March (fs) by Richard Longfield, p/c Yavapai College

ARKANSAS

ARKANSAS STATE UNIVERSITY, Jonesboro

Hail to ASU (am) by Harold Manor, p/c not listed

ASU Loyalty (fs) by George Hodge, p/c not listed

HARDING UNIVERSITY, Searcy

Harding University Alma Mater (am) by L. O. Sanderson, p/c not listed

Harding University Fight Song (fs) by G. F. Baggett, p/c not listed

HENDERSON STATE UNIVERSITY, Arkadelphia

Reddie Spirit (fs) (Tune, Give Me That Old Time Religion, refer to Song Sources, adapted Evanson), p/c not listed

Henderson Fight Song (o), no w/m credit given, arr. Evanson, p/c not listed

OUACHITA BAPTIST UNIVERSITY, Arkadelphia

Ouachita (am) no w/m credit given, p/c not listed

Fight Song (fs) by W. F. McBeth, p/c not listed

SOUTHERN BAPTIST COLLEGE, Walnut Ridge

Southern (am) by W. J. McDaniel, p/c Southern Baptist College

UNIVERSITY OF ARKANSAS, Fayetteville

University of Arkansas Hymn (am) by Brodie Payne (w) and Henry Doughty Tovey (m), p/c (c) [1911] by Henry Doughty Tovey

Arkansas Fight (fs) by Joel Leach, p/c Southern Music Publishers, p/c PD

UNIVERSITY OF ARKANSAS, Little Rock

UALR Spirit (am) by John Gray (w) and Robert Boury (m), p/c Dr. Robert Boury, Dept. of Music, University of Arkansas, Little Rock (c) [1987]

UNIVERSITY OF ARKANSAS, Monticello

UAM All Hail (am) (Tune, Annie Lisle, refer to Song Sources)
UAM Fight Song (fs) (Tune, Pony Battle Cry, refer to Song Sources)

UNIVERSITY OF ARKANSAS, Pine Bluff

Alma Mater (am) (Tune, The Old Oaken Bucket, refer to Song Sources)

UNIVERSITY OF CENTRAL ARKANSAS, Conway

Alma Mater (am), no w/m credit given, p/c not listed

UNIVERSITY OF THE OZARKS, Clarksville

Alma Mater (am) (Tune, Annie Lisle, refer to Song Sources)
Wildcat Victory (fs) by William Moffit, p/c Hal Leonard Publications

CALIFORNIA

ALLAN HANCOCK COLLEGE, Santa Maria

Hancock Alma Mater (am) by Barbara Obermeyer (w) and Robert March (m), arr. Chris Kuzell, p/c Alan Hancock College

Hancock Fight Song (fs) by R. L. Thomas, arr. Chris Kuzell, p/c Allan Hancock College

CALIFORNIA BAPTIST COLLEGE, Riverside

Alma Mater (am) by S. E. Boyd Smith, arr. D. Shannon, p/c California Baptist College

CALIFORNIA INSTITUTE OF TECHNOLOGY, Pasadena

Anthem (am) by M. M. Barnes, p/c not listed

Men of Calteck or Men of Caltech (fs) by M. M. Barnes, p/c not listed

CALIFORNIA LUTHERAN UNIVERSITY, Thousand Oaks

Alma Mater (am) (Tune, La Gaza Ladra by Rossini), Orville Dahly (wa), arr. Elmer Ramsey, p/c not listed

Hail the Kingsmen (fs) by Dr. C. Robert Zimmerman, arr. Elmer Ramsey, p/c Hollis Music Publishers

CLU Fight Song (ofs) by Dr. C. Robert Zimmerman (w) and Elmer Ramsey (m), p/c Hollis Music Publishers

CLU Loyalty Song (o) by Dr. C. Robert Zimmerman (w) and Elmer Ramsey (m), p/c Hollis Music Publishers

LU Sweetheart Song (o) by Dr. C. Robert Zimmerman (w) and Elmer Ramsey (m), p/c Hollis Music Publishers

CALIFORNIA POLYTECHNIC STATE UNIVERSITY, San Luis Obispo

All Hail, Green and Gold (am) by Harold P. Davidson, p/c not listed

Ride High You Mustangs (fs) by H. P. Davidson, arr. John Higgins, p/c not listed

Send Out a Cheer (o) by H. P. Davidson, arr. John Higgins, p/c not listed

Yea Poly (o) by H. P. Davidson, arr. John Higgins, p/c not listed

CALIFORNIA STATE POLYTECHNIC UNIVERSITY, Pomona

All Hail Green and Gold (am) by Keith Weeks, p/c not listed

Bronco Fight Song (fs) by Keith Weeks, arr. Philip Browne, p/c not listed

Inaugural Procession [official ceremonial commencement piece] (o) by Philip Browne, p/c not listed

CALIFORNIA STATE UNIVERSITY, Chico

Alma Mater (am) (Tune, Finlandia, refer to Song Sources)

Fight Song (fs) (Tune, NC-4 March, refer to Song Sources), p/c PD

CALIFORNIA STATE UNIVERSITY, Dominguez Hills

Alma Mater (am), no w/m credit given, p/c not listed

CALIFORNIA STATE UNIVERSITY, Fresno

To Thee, Our Alma Mater (am) by Charles Dana Gibson (w) and Jas. H. Morrison (m), arr. A. G. Wahlberg, p/c California State University at Fresno

Fight! Varsity! (fs) by Chet Enos (w) and Cuyler H. Leonard (m), p/c not listed

CALIFORNIA STATE UNIVERSITY, Fullerton

Titan's Home and Pride (am) [Written in 1984 as class projects, words by an English 304 (Creative Writing) class; music by a Music 422 (Composition) class under the direction of Prof. Rodger Vaughan], arr. Mark Garrabrant, p/c not listed

Titan War Chant (fs) (Tune, Win for Akron, refer to Song Sources), arr. Mark Garrabrant, p/c not listed

CALIFORNIA STATE UNIVERSITY, Hayward

Alma Mater (am) by Fry (w) and Kjelson (m), p/c not listed

Pioneer Fight Song (fs) by Cory, p/c not listed

CALIFORNIA STATE UNIVERSITY, Long Beach

Solid Men to the Front (fs) by John Philip Sousa, p/c Schirmer

CSULB Alma Mater (am) by Leon Dallin, p/c not listed

CALIFORNIA STATE UNIVERSITY, Los Angeles

University Hymn (am) (Tune, St. Anne, refer to Song Sources)

CALIFORNIA STATE UNIVERSITY, Northridge

Hail to the Matadors (am) by Richard Kaufman, p/c Richard Kaufman

CSUN Fight Song (fs) by Richard Kaufman, p/c Richard Kaufman

CALIFORNIA STATE UNIVERSITY, Sacramento

CSUS Alma Mater (am) by Don T. McDonald, p/c not listed

CSUS Fight Song (fs) by Don T. McDonald, p/c not listed

CALIFORNIA STATE UNIVERSITY, San Jose

Hail, Spartans Hail (am) by Gerald Erwin, arr. Brent Heisinger, p/c not listed

Down from Under (fs) by Darrell Graves, p/c not listed

Fight On Spartans (ofs) by Dr. Gus Lease (w) and Frank Erickson (m), p/c not listed

San Jose State Fight Song (ofs) by Jack Wiles, p/c not listed

COLLEGE OF NOTRE DAME, Belmont

Alma Mater (am) by Sr. Rosemarie Gavin (w) and Dr. Birgitte Moyer (m), p/c College of Notre Dame (c) [1977]

EL CAMINO COLLEGE, via Torrance

El Camino Alma Mater (am) by Jack Ledbetter (w) and W. W. Flewelling, Jr. (m), p/c El Camino College, other arrangers: Crist Mikkelsen (Men's Glee Club), Tom Owens (Men's Glee Club), Calvin Greer (Marching Band)

E.C.C. Fight Song (fs) by Joan Hosking, p/c El Camino College

LA VERNE UNIVERSITY, La Verne

Alma Mater Hymn (am) by Hellenberg and Funderburgh, arr. Fahringer, p/c La Verne University

Fight Song (fs) (Tune, Washington and Lee Swing, refer to Song Sources)

MILLS COLLEGE, Oakland

Fires of Wisdom (am), no w/m credit given, p/c not listed

MOUNT ST. MARY'S COLLEGE, Los Angeles

Alma Mater (am) by Amedee Tremblay, p/c Mt. St. Mary's College

Hymn to Mount St. Mary's (o) by Dr. Will Garroway, p/c Mt. St. Mary's College

ORANGE COAST COLLEGE, Costa Mesa

Go Pirates (fs) by Paul Cox, p/c not listed

Parade of the Pirates (ofs) by Paul Cox, p/c not listed

PACIFIC UNION COLLEGE, Angwin

Our College on the Mountain (am) by George H. Jeys (w) and Margaret Vollmer (m), p/c not listed

RIO HONDO COLLEGE, Whittier

Rio Hondo (am) by Lar Best, arr. Jacobs, p/c Rio Hondo College

Rio Hondo Fight Song (fs) (Tune, Touchdown by Paul Yoder), p/c Sam Fox

Push Song (o) by Lar Best, arr. Jacobs, p/c Rio Hondo College

SACRAMENTO CITY COLLEGE, Sacramento

Fight Song (fs) (Tune, Mighty Oregon by Gilbert), p/c Edwin H. Morris & Co.

SACRAMENTO STATE UNIVERSITY, Sacramento

Fight, Hornets, Fight (fs) by McDonald and Riddle, p/c not listed

SADDLEBACK COLLEGE, Mission Viejo

El Gaucho (fs) by Jack Sheaton, p/c Saddleback College

SAN DIEGO STATE UNIVERSITY, San Diego

Hail, Montezuma (am), no w/m credit given, p/c not listed

Fite On Aztecs (fs) by Losey, p/c Mills Music

Monty's Jump (o), no w/m credit given, p/c not listed

Quetzacoatl (o), no w/m credit given, p/c not listed

SAN FRANCISCO STATE UNIVERSITY, San Francisco

Alma Mater (am), (w/m) by students, p/c San Francisco State University

Hail to San Francisco State (oam) by Clarence Hall, p/c not listed

Fight Song (fs), (w/m) by students, p/c San Francisco State University

State Victory Song (ofs) by Dorothy Williamson (w) and Mildred Roof (m), p/c not listed

SAN JOSE STATE UNIVERSITY, San Jose

Hail, Spartans, Hail (am) by Gerald Erwin, arr. Scott Pierson, p/c San Jose State University

Down from Under (fs) by James Veteran (w) and Darrell Graves (m), p/c San Jose State University

San Jose State Fight Song (ofs) by Johnson Wiles, arr. Brent Heisinger, p/c San Jose State University

Spartan Fight Song (ofs), no w/m credit given, p/c not listed

Fight On Spartans (o) by Dr. Gus Lease (w) and Frank Erickson (m), p/c San Jose State University

STANFORD UNIVERSITY, Stanford

Hail Stanford Hail (am) by A.W.S. (w) and M.R.C. (m), p/c not listed

Come Join the Band (fs) (Tune, New Colonial March, refer to Song Sources), (wa) Aurania Ellerbeck, p/c not listed

UNIVERSITY OF CALIFORNIA, Berkeley

All Hail! Blue and Gold (am) by Harold W. Bingham, arr. A. Elkus, p/c not listed

California Hymn (am), (refer to All Hail! Blue and Gold)

Hail to California (oam) by Clinton R. Morse and C. Cushing, p/c not listed

Fight for California (fs) by Robert N. Fitch (wa) (Tune, Lights Out March, refer to Song Sources)

Big "C" (o) by H. P. Williams and N. McLaren, arr. W. Denny, p/c not listed

The CAL Drinking Song (o), no w/m credit given, arr. L. Austin, p/c not listed

California Indian Song (o) by H. Bingham, arr. L. Austin, p/c not listed

California We're for You (o) by T. Haley, arr. L. Austin, p/c not listed

Fight 'Em (o) by I. Kornblum and H. Kowalski, p/c not listed

Golden Bear (o) by C. Gayley, arr. J. Elkus, p/c not listed

Make Way for the Bear (o) by T. Haley, arr. L. Austin, p/c not listed

Our Golden Bear (o) (Tune, The Pope, refer to Song Sources)

Palms of Victory (o), no w/m credit given, arr. Rawlings, p/c not listed

Roll On, You Golden Bear (o) by D. Mandel and Paul Yoder, p/c not listed

St. Anne (o) by Issac Watts (w) and William Croft (m), p/c PD

Sons of California (o) by C. R. Morse, arr. L. Austin, p/c not listed

The Stanford Jonah (o) by Ted Haley, p/c PD

Toast to California (o) by J. Hunt, p/c not listed

UNIVERSITY OF CALIFORNIA, Davis

Hail to California (am) by Clinton R. Morse, arr. Charles C. Cushing

Aggie Fight (fs), no w/m credit given, arr. Larry Austin, p/c not listed

Big "C" (o) by N. S. McLaren (w) and H. P. Williams (m), arr. Larry Austin, p/c PD

Roll, Big CA, Roll (o) by Greg Sweet, arr. John Moore, p/c not listed

Sons of California (o) by C. R. Morse, p/c PD

UNIVERSITY OF CALIFORNIA (UCLA), Los Angeles

Go On, Bruins (fs) by Gordon G. Holmquist, Milo Sweet, and Gwen Sweet, p/c Edwin H. Morris & Co.

UNIVERSITY OF CALIFORNIA, Santa Barbara

Hail to California (am) by Clinton R. Morse, arr. S.A.M., p/c PD

UNIVERSITY OF CALIFORNIA, Santa Cruz

The University Hymn (am) (Tune, St. Anne by Isaac Watts [1674–1748] (w) and William Croft [1678–1727] (m) refer to Song Sources), p/c PD

UNIVERSITY OF SOUTHERN CALIFORNIA, Los Angeles

All Hail (am) by Al Wesson, arr. William A. Schaefer, p/c Sweet Music, Inc. (c) [1956]

Fight On (fs) by Milo Sweet and Glen Grant, arr. Robert Linn, p/c Sweet Music, Inc. (c) [1958]

The Cardinal and Gold (o) by Al Wesson, arr. Robert Linn, p/c not listed

Clear the Way for USC (o), no w/m credit given, p/c PD

Conquest (o) by Alfred Newman (Tune adapted from the movie *Captain of Castile*), arr. Tony Fox, p/c Fox Music (Robbins Music Corp.)

Tribute to Troy (o) by Ronald Broadwell, p/c not listed

Trojan Fanfare (o) by Tony Fox, p/c not listed

UNIVERSITY OF THE PACIFIC, Stockton

Pacific Hail (am) by Lois Warner Winston (w) and Van Schmutz (m), p/c not listed

Hungry Tigers (fs) by Bodley, arr. Finley, p/c not listed

Old Cheers (ofs) by Bodley, arr. Finley, p/c not listed

WHITTIER COLLEGE, Whittier

Whittier College Alma Mater (am) (Tune, Ua Like No A Like ("My Heart's Choice") by Alice Everett), p/c not listed

Go Poets (fs) by Roger C. Pease, p/c (c) [1964] pub. not listed.

Friends Forever (o) by Herbert and Marjorie Harris (wa) and Margaretha Lohmann (m), arr. Stephen Gothold, p/c (c) [1989], pub. not listed

Hail to Dear Old Whittier (o) by Herbert E. Collins, harmonized by Burton Arant [dedicated to Dr. Walter F. Dexter], p/c (c) [1927], pub. not listed

COLORADO

COLORADO COLLEGE, Colorado Springs

Colorado College Alma Mater (am) (Tune, Gaudeamus Igitur, refer to Song Sources)

Fight Song (fs) (Tune, Washington and Lee Swing, refer to Song Sources)

COLORADO STATE UNIVERSITY, Fort Collins

Colorado State University Alma Mater (am) by Bueche, p/c not listed

Colorado State University Fite Song (fs) by Vinke, arr. Bueche, p/c not listed

Boom Song (o) by Bueche, p/c not listed

MESA STATE COLLEGE, Grand Junction

Our Alma Mater (am), no w/m credit given, p/c not listed

SOUTHERN COLORADO STATE COLLEGE, Pueblo

Old S.C. (am) by B. Kelly, arr. G. Roach, p/c not listed

Stand Up and Cheer (fs) (Tune, Stand Up and Cheer, refer to Song Sources)

UNITED STATES AIR FORCE ACADEMY, Colorado Springs

Toast to the Host (am) by Robert M. Crawford, p/c Carl Fischer, Inc. [1931]

Go, Falcons (fs) by Vincent, p/c not listed

The U.S. Air Force (ofs) by Robert M. Crawford, p/c Carl Fischer, Inc. [1939]

Big Blue (o) by Vincent, p/c not listed

Falcons Fight (o) by Vincent, p/c not listed

UNIVERSITY OF COLORADO, Boulder

University of Colorado Alma Mater (am) by J.D.A. Oghilvy (w) and Hugh E. McMillen (m), p/c Allen Intercollegiate Music, Inc.

Fight CU, Down the Field (fs) by Richard Durnett (w), Culver Military Institute (m), p/c PD

Glory, Glory Colorado (o) (Tune, Glory, Glory Hallelujah, refer to Song Sources)

Go Colorado (o) by Bill Simon, p/c Carl Fischer, Inc. (c) [1957]

UNIVERSITY OF COLORADO, Denver

Alma Mater (am), no w/m credit given, p/c not listed

UNIVERSITY OF DENVER, Denver

We Wear Our Colors, Red and Gold (o), no w/m credit given, p/c PD

UNIVERSITY OF NORTHERN COLORADO, Greeley

Ah, Well I Remember (am) by J. D. Forrest Cline, p/c not listed

Fight Song (fs), no w/m credit given, p/c not listed

UNIVERSITY OF SOUTHERN COLORADO, Pueblo

Alma Mater (am), no w/m credit given, p/c not listed

WESTERN STATE COLLEGE OF COLORADO, Gunnison

Western State Fight Song (fs) by Robert Hawkins, p/c Neil A. Kjos Music Company

CONNECTICUT

CENTRAL CONNECTICUT STATE UNIVERSITY, New Britain

CCSU Alma Mater (am), no w/m credit given, p/c not listed

CCSU Fight Song (fs), no w/m credit given, p/c not listed

CCSU Victory (o), no w/m credit given, p/c not listed

CONNECTICUT COLLEGE, New London

Alma Mater by the Sea (am), no w/m credit given, p/c not listed

FAIRFIELD UNIVERSITY, Fairfield

Alma Mater (am), no w/m credit given, p/c not listed

When the Stags Come Marching In (fs) (Tune, When the Saints Go Marching In, refer to Song Sources)

QUINNIPIAC COLLEGE, Hamden

Quinnipiac Alma Mater (am) by Frank V. Bigelow, p/c not listed

SOUTHERN CONNECTICUT STATE UNIVERSITY, New Haven

Alma Mater (am) (Tune, Finlandia, refer to Song Sources)

Victory (fs) by A. H. Larsen, p/c not listed

TRINITY COLLEGE, Hartford

'Neath the Elms (am) by A. P. Burgwin (w), no (m) credit given, p/c not listed

Fight Trinity (fs) by Harry W. Nordstrom, p/c not listed

UNITED STATES COAST GUARD ACADEMY, New London

Coast Guard Alma Mater (am) by Arthur Bryer, arr. William Mc-Peters, p/c not listed

Semper Paratus (fs) (also of Coast Guard) by Capt. Francis Van Boskereck (refer to Song Sources)

UNIVERSITY OF BRIDGEPORT, Bridgeport

Alma Mater (am) by Albert Dickason, arr. Harold Dart, p/c not listed

For U.B. (fs) no w/m credit given, p/c not listed

Be You for U.B. (ofs), no w/m credit given, p/c not listed

UNIVERSITY OF CONNECTICUT, Storrs

Old Connecticut (am) by Alice Davis, p/c not listed

U Conn Husky (fs) by Herbert France, p/c not listed

UNIVERSITY OF HARTFORD, West Hartford

University of Hartford Alma Mater (am) by Joseph H. Soifer '46, p/c not listed

Hartford On to Victory (fs), no w/m credit given, p/c not listed

UNIVERSITY OF NEW HAVEN, West Haven

Let Us Remember (am) (Tune, an old Welsh air), Alexis Sommers (wa), arr. Michael Kaloyanides, p/c PD

Fight Song (fs) (Tune, Our Heritage March, refer to Song Sources), arr. Albert Celotto, p/c C. L. Barnhouse Co.

YALE UNIVERSITY, New Haven

Bright College Years (am) by Carl Wilhelm, p/c PD

Down the Field (fs) (refer to Song Sources)

The Bull Dog (ofs) (also Bull Dog! Bull Dog! Bow, Wow, Wow) by Cole Porter, (c) [1911], p/c PD

Yale Boola (ofs) by A. M. Hirsch, p/c PD

Adeline, the Yale Boola Girl (o) by A. M. Hirsch, p/c PD

Alma Mater (o) by Jos. G. Shepard, p/c PD

Brave Mother Yale (o) by Thomas P. Shepard, p/c PD

Come Rally Tonight (o), no w/m credit given, p/c PD

Dear Old Yale (o) (Tune, Die Wacht am Rhein, refer to Song Sources)

Les Charmes de New Haven (o) by Chas. M. King, p/c PD

Little Knot of Blue (o) by Thos. G. Shepard, p/c PD

Lux et Veritas - Reunion Song (o) by Leonard M. Thomas '01, p/c PD

Miss Harvard of Yale (o) by Harry von Tilzer, p/c PD

'Neath the Elms of Dear Old Yale (o), no w/m credit given, p/c PD

Ode for Commencement Day at Yale University [1895] (o) by Horatio W. Parker, p/c PD

Only an Hour (o) by S. Weinz, p/c PD

The Scotchman (o), no w/m credit given

Where the Elm Tree Grows (o), no w/m credit given, p/c PD

Yale College Quickstep (o) by P. A. Smith, p/c PD

DELAWARE

UNIVERSITY OF DELAWARE, Newark

Alma Mater (am) by A. S. Loudis, arr. King, p/c not listed

Delaware Fight Song (fs) by George F. Kelly, arr. King, p/c not listed

Delaware Forever (o) (Tune, University of Pennsylvania Band March, refer to Song Sources)

DISTRICT OF COLUMBIA

CATHOLIC UNIVERSITY OF AMERICA, Washington, DC

CU Alma Mater (am) by Thos. J. McLean, band arr. G. T. Jones, voice arr. Reagan, p/c not listed

The Flying Cardinals (fs) by Paul D. H. Lehman, p/c Paul D. H. Lehman

GEORGE WASHINGTON UNIVERSITY, Washington, DC

Hail George Washington (am) by George Roth, p/c George Washington University

Buff and Blue (fs) by Eugene Sweeney, p/c George Washington University

GEORGETOWN UNIVERSITY, Washington, DC

Hail! O Georgetown (am) by Robert Collier (wa), (Tune, March of the Men of Harlech, refer to Song Sources)

Georgetown Fight Song (fs), no w/m credit given, p/c not listed

The Sons of Georgetown (o), no w/m credit given, p/c PD

HOWARD UNIVERSITY, Washington, DC

Alma Mater (am) by J. H. Brooks (w) and F. D. Malone (m), p/c not listed

IMMACULATA COLLEGE OF WASHINGTON, Washington, DC

Immaculata (am) by Sister Marian Thomas Kinney, S.P. (w) and Sister Annette Cecile Holmes, S.P. (m), p/c Immaculata College of Washington

FLORIDA

BETHUNE-COOKMAN COLLEGE, Daytona Beach

BCC Alma Mater (am), no w/m credit given, p/c not listed

CENTRAL FLORIDA COMMUNITY COLLEGE, Ocala

CFCC Alma Mater (am) by James Myatt and Gene A. Lawton, arr. Gene A. Lawton, p/c Central Florida Community College

CHIPOLA JUNIOR COLLEGE, Marianna

By the Banks of Old Chipola (am) (Tune, Annie Lisle, refer to Song Sources)

EDISON COMMUNITY COLLEGE, Fort Myers

Edison, On Edison (am) by Daniel C. Henderson (w/m), p/c not listed

FLORIDA AGRICULTURAL AND MECHANICAL UNIVERSITY, Tallahassee

FAMU Alma Mater (am), no w/m credit given, arr. Powers, p/c not listed

Florida Song (oam), no w/m credit given, arr. Powers, p/c not listed

Mighty Rattlers (fs), no w/m credit given, arr. Edwards, p/c not listed

I'm from FAMU (ofs), no w/m credit given, arr. Powers, p/c not listed

Ole FAMU Spirit (ofs), no w/m credit given, arr. Powers, p/c not listed

Our Florida (ofs), no w/m credit given, p/c not listed

FLORIDA ATLANTIC UNIVERSITY, Boca Raton

Florida Atlantic University Alma Mater (am) by C. Clark Bell (w/m), arr. Bob Nicholson, p/c Florida Atlantic University

Fight Song (fs) by Clark Bell (w/m), arr. Bill Prince, p/c PD

FLORIDA INTERNATIONAL UNIVERSITY, Miami

Alma Mater (am), no w/m credit given, p/c not listed

FLORIDA SOUTHERN COLLEGE, Lakeland

Alma Mater (am) (Tune, Annie Lisle, refer to Song Sources)

Go Mocs, Go (fs) by Wells, p/c not listed

FLORIDA STATE UNIVERSITY, Tallahassee

High O'er the Towering Pines (am) by Johnny Lawrence (w/m), arr. Charles Carter, p/c not listed [1949]

FSU Fight Song (fs) by Doug Alley (w) and Tommy Wright (m), arr. Charles Carter, p/c not listed [1950]

Hymn to the Garnet and the Gold (o) by J. Dayton Smith (w/m), arr. Charles Carter, p/c not listed

JACKSONVILLE UNIVERSITY, Jacksonville

JU Alma Mater (am) by Sackman, p/c not listed

JU Fight Song (fs) by A. E. Rogers, p/c by Belwin/Mills

JU Hymn (o) by William Koskins, p/c not listed

JU Processional (o) by William Hoskins, p/c not listed

PENSACOLA JUNIOR COLLEGE, Pensacola

PJC Alma Mater (am) by John Venetozzi, arr. John Venetozzi, p/c not listed

Fight Song (fs) (Tune, On Wisconsin, refer to Song Sources)

ROLLINS COLLEGE, Winter Park

Set Like a Gem (am) by Rose Mills Powers (w) and Homer Stanley Pope (m), p/c Angel Alley Press [1927]

Rollins Rouser (fs) (Tune, Ohio Wesleyan Song), Rena Sheffield (wa), p/c not listed

SAINT LEO COLLEGE, Saint Leo

Saint Leo Alma Mater (am) by Zaitz (w) and Salvatore (m), p/c not listed

STETSON UNIVERSITY, DeLand

Stetson Alma Mater (am) by Flemming, arr. Hulley, p/c not listed

Go-Hatters-Go! (fs) by Richard Feasel, p/c Sam Fox Publishing Co.

UNIVERSITY OF FLORIDA, Gainesville

Alma Mater (am) by Milton Yeats, arr. Reid Poole, p/c Broadcast Music, Inc.

Orange and Blue (fs) by Allen, arr. Poole, p/c not listed

UNIVERSITY OF MIAMI, Coral Gables

Alma Mater (am) by Lampe and Asdurian, arr. Henry Fillmore, p/c University of Miami

Hail to the Spirit of Miami U (fs) by Clark and Kennedy, arr. Henry Fillmore, p/c University Bands

UNIVERSITY OF SOUTH FLORIDA, Tampa

USF Alma Mater (am) by R. Wayne Hugoboom, arr. Gale Sperry, p/c University of South Florida

Golden Brahman Fight Song (fs) by Gale Sperry, p/c University of South Florida

GEORGIA

ATLANTA UNIVERSITY, Atlanta

Alma Mater (am), no w/m credit given, p/c not listed

AUGUSTA COLLEGE, Augusta

Where Sentinels Once Guarded (am) by Eugenia Toole, p/c not listed

EMORY UNIVERSITY, Atlanta

Emory Alma Mater (am) by Sally Stewart (w), no (m) credit given, p/c not listed

GEORGIA COLLEGE, Milledgeville

Alma Mater, Teacher, Friend (am) by Ruth Sandiford Garrard, p/c Georgia College

GEORGIA INSTITUTE OF TECHNOLOGY, Atlanta

Georgia Tech Alma Mater (am) by Frank Roman, p/c Frank Roman

The Ramblin' Wreck from Georgia Tech (fs) by Frank Roman, p/c Edwin H. Morris & Co.

Georgia Tech Yellow Jackets (o) by Frank Roman, p/c Frank Roman

Up with the White and Gold (o) by Frank Roman, p/c Frank Roman

GEORGIA SOUTHERN COLLEGE, Statesboro

Alma Mater (am) (Tune, Annie Lisle, refer to Song Sources)

GEORGIA STATE UNIVERSITY, Atlanta

GSU Alma Mater (am) (Tune, Ode to Joy, refer to Song Sources), Kenneth England, Prof. Emeritus of English (wa), p/c not listed

KENNESAW STATE COLLEGE, Marietta

Kennesaw State College Alma Mater (am) (Tune, Gaudeamus Igitur, refer to Song Sources)

MORRIS BROWN COLLEGE, Atlanta

Morris Brown College Alma Mater (am), no w/m credit given, p/c not listed

NORTH GEORGIA COLLEGE, Dahlonega

Proudly We Hail Thee (am) by Desmond Booth, p/c North Georgia College

UNIVERSITY OF GEORGIA, Athens

Alma Mater (am) by J. B. Wright, Jr., p/c University of Georgia

Glory, Glory to Old Georgia (fs) (Tune, Battle Hymn of the Republic, refer to Song Sources), 6/8 version adaptation G. W. Walter, p/c University of Georgia

Hail to Georgia (o) by G. W. Walter, p/c University of Georgia

VALDOSTA STATE COLLEGE, Valdosta

Alma Mater (am) (Tune, Annie Lisle, refer to Song Sources), Helen Allen Thomas and Evelyn Brown (wa), arr. Dr. John Huxford, p/c not listed

WESLEYAN COLLEGE, Macon

Hail Wesleyan (am) by James R. Gillette, p/c not listed

WEST GEORGIA COLLEGE, Carrollton

Alma Mater (am) by Felton Dunn (s) and Bruce Borton (m), p/c not listed

HAWAII

BRIGHAM YOUNG UNIVERSITY, Laie, Oahu

Hail Alma Mater (am) (Tune, music by Brahms, title not listed), Joseph Spurrier (w), p/c not listed

BYUH Fight Song (fs), no w/m credit given, p/c not listed

CHAMINADE UNIVERSITY, Honolulu

Chaminade Alma Mater, Hail (am) by Joseph A. Becker, S. M. (w) and John S. McCreary (m), p/c not listed

UNIVERSITY OF HAWAII, Hilo

Pulelo Ha'aheo (am) by Kauanoe Kamana, Kalena Silva, and Pila Wilson (w), Takeo Kudo (m), p/c Takeo Kudo [1987]

UNIVERSITY OF HAWAII, Honolulu

In Green Manoa Valley (am) by May Gay, arr. Richard Lum, p/c not listed

Fight for Old Hawaii (fs) by Don George, arr. Bill Kaneda, p/c not listed

Hawaii Five-O (o) (Tune, Hawaii Five-O, refer to Song Sources)

Hawaiian War Chant (o) (Tune, Hawaiian War Chant (o), refer to Song Sources)

Here's to Our Dear Hawaii (o) by J. S. Zamecnik, p/c Sam Fox Publishing Co.

UNIVERSITY OF HAWAII AT MANOA, Honolulu

University of Hawaii Alma Mater (am), no w/m credit given, p/c not listed

Co-Ed (fs), no w/m credit given, p/c not listed

IDAHO

IDAHO STATE UNIVERSITY, Pocatello

ISU Alma Mater Hymn (am) by Wesley M. Harris, arr. Wesley M. Harris, p/c not listed

Growl Bengals, Growl (fs) by Jay Slaughter and Del Slaughter, p/c not listed

NORTHWEST NAZARENE COLLEGE, Nampa

Hail to NNC (am), no w/m credit given, p/c not listed

On Crusaders (fs) (Tune, On Wisconsin, refer to Song Sources)

RICKS COLLEGE, Rexburg

Happy Ties (am) (Tune, Annie Lisle, refer to Song Sources), Ezra C. Dalby [early college president] (wa), p/c not listed

Vikings Fight (fs) by Del Slaughter, p/c not listed

UNIVERSITY OF IDAHO, Moscow

Go, Vandals (fs) by O'Donnell, arr. Billingsley, p/c University of Idaho

Here We Have Idaho (o) by MacKinley Helm, arr. Billingsley, p/c University of Idaho

ILLINOIS

AURORA UNIVERSITY, Aurora

Aurora (am), no w/m credit given, arr. Georgia Angevine, p/c Aurora University

BLACK HAWK COLLEGE, Moline

Black Hawk College Loyalty (am) by R. Keeley, arr. D. Moe, p/c Black Hawk College

BRADLEY UNIVERSITY, Peoria

Hail, Red and White (am) by Fred W. Thompson, arr. Dean C. Howard, p/c not listed

Charge On, Bradley (fs), no w/m credit given, arr. Dean C. Howard, p/c not listed

Bradley Loyalty Song (ofs) by John Fritz and Frederick Siebert, p/c not listed

Injun Musik (ofs) by Dean C. Howard, p/c not listed

COLLEGE OF ST. FRANCIS, Joliet

Alma Mater (am) by Helen Coughlin (w) and Clare Greenwood (m), p/c College of St. Francis

College Chimes (o) by Daniel Lord, S. J. (w) and John Quinn, S. J. (m), p/c College of St. Francis

DE PAUL UNIVERSITY, Chicago

De Paul Victory Song (fs) by J. Leo Sullivan (w) and A. C. Becker (m), arr. Gingrich, p/c not listed

EASTERN ILLINOIS UNIVERSITY, Charleston

Alma Mater (am) by George Westcott, p/c not listed

Eastern Loyalty (fs) by Earl Boyd, p/c Eastern Illinois University

Go Eastern, Go (o) by George Westcott, p/c not listed

ELMHURST COLLEGE, Elmhurst

Alma Mater (am) (Tune, Annie Lisle, refer to Song Sources)

Fight Song (fs) (Tune, Our Director March, refer to Song Sources)

GREENVILLE COLLEGE, Greenville

Alma Mater (am) (Tune, Annie Lisle, refer to Song Sources)

Fight Song (fs) (Tune, Our Director March, refer to Song Sources)

ILLINOIS BENEDICTINE COLLEGE, Lisle

Eagle Fight Song (fs) by Carmen Kocian, p/c not listed. (This song was proposed after the college changed its name from St. Procopius to Illinois Benedictine College in 1971. However, Illinois Benedictine College does not have, at the present time, either an official fight song or an official alma mater hymn.)

When the school was named St. Procopius, the following songs were used:

Fight Song (fs) no w/m credit given, p/c not listed (c) [1930s]

Side by Side (ofs), no w/m credit given, p/c not listed (c) [1930s]

Dear Old Lisle (o) by A. Comlossy (w), no (m) credit given, p/c not listed

Procopius (o) by Francis J. Sindelar, p/c Francis J. Sindelar, St. Procopius College, Lisle, IL (c) [1920s]

ILLINOIS CENTRAL COLLEGE, East Peoria

ICC Alma Mater (am) by Richard Richardson, arr. Donald Lewellen, p/c Illinois Central College

ILLINOIS COLLEGE, Jacksonville

Illinois College Alma Mater (am) by Ruth and Boyd Pixley, p/c not listed

Fight Song (fs) (Tune, Washington and Lee Swing, refer to Song Sources)

ILLINOIS STATE UNIVERSITY, Normal

Glory Hast Thou (am) (Tune, Deutschland Uber Alles, refer to Song Sources)

Redbirds Marching Song (fs) by Fletcher, arr. Foeller, p/c not listed

ILLINOIS WESLEYAN UNIVERSITY, Bloomington

Tribute to Wesleyan (o) by R. C. Smedley, p/c PD

KNOX COLLEGE, Galesburg

The Purple and the Gold (o), no w/m credit given, p/c PD

LAKE FOREST COLLEGE, Lake Forest

Lake Forest College Song (o), no w/m credit given, p/c PD

LOYOLA UNIVERSITY, Chicago

Alma Mater (am), no w/m credit given, p/c not listed

MCKENDREE COLLEGE, Lebanon

Alma Mater (am), no w/m credit given, p/c not listed

Lebanon Music (o) (Tune, O Tannenbaum, refer to Song Sources), p/c not listed

McKendree, We All Love Her So (o) by Hurt (w) and Wm. R. Harris (m), p/c McKendree College

MILLIKIN UNIVERSITY, Decatur

Alma Mater (am) by R. Schueler, p/c not listed

Fight for the Blue (fs), no w/m credit given, p/c not listed

NORTH PARK COLLEGE AND THEOLOGICAL SEMINARY, Chicago

Alma Mater (am) by Milton Strom, p/c not listed

North Park Victory (fs), no w/m credit given, arr. Wesley Hanson, p/c not listed

NORTHEASTERN ILLINOIS UNIVERSITY, Chicago

Northeastern Alma Mater (am) by Harlech, arr. W. T. Bradley, p/c Commissioned by Phi Mu Alpha Sinfonia (Chi Omega Chapter) for Northeastern Illinois University

Go Golden Eagles (fs) (Tune, Washington and Lee Swing, refer to Song Sources)

NORTHERN ILLINOIS UNIVERSITY, De Kalb

Alma Mater (am) by A. N. Annas, p/c not listed

NIU Fight Song (fs) by Erickson, p/c not listed

NORTHWESTERN UNIVERSITY, Evanston

Alma Mater (am) (Tune, Quaecumque Sunt Vera by Joseph Haydn), p/c PD

Go U Northwestern (fs) by Theo. C. Van Etten, arr. Harry Alford, p/c Edwin H. Morris & Co.

Cheer for the Purple (o), no w/m credit given, p/c not listed

Northwestern Push Song (o) by Roberston, arr. Harry Alford, p/c Edwin H. Morris & Co.

OLIVET NAZARENE UNIVERSITY, Kankakee

Alma Mater (am) by Byron Carmony, p/c Olivet Nazarene University

PRINCIPIA COLLEGE, Elsah

Principia Hymn (am) by Winifred Hubbell, p/c Principia College

QUINCY COLLEGE, Quincy

High Above the Mississippi (am) (Tune, Annie Lisle, refer to Song Sources)

Quincy College Fight Song (fs) by Rev. Daniel, arr. Charles R. Winking, p/c not listed

ROCKFORD COLLEGE, Rockford

Decus et Veritas (am) (Tune, Annie Lisle, refer to Song Sources), p/c no (w) credit given, appears in *Songs of Rockford College,* Rockford, Ill.: Rockford College, 1954.

SOUTHERN ILLINOIS UNIVERSITY, Carbondale

Southern Alma Mater (am) by Grover Clarke Morgan, p/c Southern Illinois University

Go Southern, Go (fs) by Grover Clarke Morgan, p/c Southern Illinois University

SIU Loyalty (o) by Glenn Cliff Bainum, p/c Southern Illinois University

UNIVERSITY OF CHICAGO, Chicago

Alma Mater (am), no w/m credit given, p/c PD

For Chicago Alma Mater (oam) by Donald R. Richberg, p/c PD

Wave the Flag (fs) by Gordon Erickson, p/c Edwin H. Morris & Co.

John D. Rockefeller (o), no w/m credit given, p/c PD

Maroon (o) by Donald R. Richberg, p/c PD

University Quick Step (o) by E. M. Shaw, p/c PD

UNIVERSITY OF ILLINOIS, Urbana/Champaign

Hail to the Orange (am), no w/m credit given, p/c not listed

Illinois Loyalty (fs) by Guild, p/c Edwin H. Morris & Co.

Illinois (o) by Walter Howe Jones, p/c PD

Oskee-Wow-Wow (o), no w/m credit given, p/c not listed

Pride of the Illini (o) by Karl King, p/c Karl L. King Music House

WAUBONSEE COLLEGE, Sugar Grove

Waubonsee Fight Song (fs) by Howard Akers and Duane Wickiser, arr. Duane Wickiser, p/c Waubonsee College

WESTERN ILLINOIS UNIVERSITY, Macomb

Western Loyalty (am) by Walter P. Morgan (w) and Harold F. Schory (m), p/c not listed

We're Marching On (fs), no w/m credit given, p/c not listed

WHEATON COLLEGE, Wheaton

Alma Mater, Wheaton College (am) (Tune, Orange and Black, refer to Song Sources)

Orange and Blue Fight Song (fs) by Robert Loveless, arr. Arthur Katterjohn, p/c not listed

Laureata (o) by Elliott G. Coleman, p/c not listed

INDIANA

ANDERSON UNIVERSITY, Anderson

Anderson, Our Alma Mater (am) (Tune, Annie Lisle, refer to Song Sources)

Soar Ravens, Soar (fs), no w/m credit given, p/c Anderson University

BALL STATE UNIVERSITY, Muncie

BSU Alma Mater (am) by Gladys Shindler Cheisman, arr. Higgins, p/c not listed

Fight Team, Fight (fs) by Carl Hofer, arr. Higgins, p/c not listed

BETHEL COLLEGE, Mishawaka

Alma Mater (am) by Marvin G. Baker, arr. Donald R. Murray, p/c Bethel College

To God Be the Glory (o) by Fanny J. Crosby (w) and William H. Doane (m), p/c Paragon Associates, Inc.

BUTLER UNIVERSITY, Indianapolis

Gallery of Memories (am) by Fred W. Wolff, arr. Mike Leckrone, p/c Butler University

Butler War Song (fs) by Heiney, arr. Charles Heinzie and Mike Leckrone, p/c Butler University

Back to Butler (o) by Joel Marsh, arr. Mike Leckrone and Bob Grechscy, p/c Butler University

Fight On (o) by Joel Marsh, arr. Mike Leckrone, p/c Butler University

DE PAUW UNIVERSITY, Greencastle

De Pauw Toast (am) by Vivian Bard, arr. Jerry Owen, p/c De Pauw University

Here's to De Pauw (fs) (Tune, Down the Line, refer to Song Sources)

In Praise of Old De Pauw (o) by Carl Langlotz, (Tune, possibly, Old Nassau [Princeton], refer to Song Sources), p/c PD

HANOVER COLLEGE, Hanover

Hail, Alma Mater (am) by Mrs. Parker (w) and Meredith Willson (m), p/c Hanover College

Hanover—We're for You (fs) by Clara B. Ulen, arr. Wm. W. Taylor, p/c Clara B. Ulen, Hanover College, Alumni Association

INDIANA STATE UNIVERSITY, Terre Haute

Alma Mater (am) (Tune, Annie Lisle, refer to Song Sources)

March On, Sycamores! (fs) by J. A. Gremellspacher, p/c not listed

INDIANA UNIVERSITY, Bloomington

Hail to Old IU (am) (Tune, Amici, refer to Song Sources)

Indiana, Our Indiana (fs) by Russell P. Harker (w) and Karl L. King (m), p/c Edwin H. Morris & Co.

Chimes of Indiana (o) by Hoagy Carmichael, p/c Indiana Union and Southern Music Co.

Indiana Fight (o) by Leroy C. Hinkle, p/c PD

Indiana Loyalty (o) by Mark Hindsley, p/c Indiana Union and Mark Hindsley

INDIANA UNIVERSITY, South Bend

Hail to Old IU (am) (Tune, Amici, refer to Song Sources)

INDIANA UNIVERSITY SOUTHEAST, New Albany

Hail to Old IU (am) (Tune, Amici, refer to Song Sources), Joe T. Giles (wa)

MANCHESTER COLLEGE, North Manchester

By the Keipnapocomoco (am) (Tune, Annie Lisle, refer to Song Sources), p/c Mrs. George Beauchamp (wa), p/c not listed

Manchester College, Hail to Thee (fs), no w/m credit

MARION COLLEGE, Marion

Cheer, Cheer for Marion College (am), no w/m credit given, p/c not listed

Titans Fight Song (fs) by Corliss, arr. Welch, p/c not listed

PURDUE UNIVERSITY, West Lafayette

The Purdue Hymn (am), no w/m credit given, p/c not listed

Hail Purdue (fs) by J. Morrison (w) and E. J. Wotawa (m), arr. Harry Alford, p/c Edwin H. Morris & Co.

Back to Old Purdue (o) by Davis and Reel, arr. Harry Alford, p/c Edwin H. Morris & Co.

Fighting Varsity (o) by Emrick, arr. Harry Alford, p/c Edwin H. Morris & Co.

For the Honor of Old Purdue (o) by Huston, arr. Paul Yoder, p/c Edwin H. Morris & Co.

Vive Purdue (o) by J. C. Arthur, p/c PD

ROSE-HULMAN INSTITUTE OF TECHNOLOGY, Terre Haute

Dear Old Rose (am) (Tune, Gerstmeyer, a local high school song, source information not available), p/c not listed

SAINT JOSEPH'S COLLEGE, Rensselaer

Saints in Concert (fs) (Tune, Saints in Concert ["d" to end], refer to Song Sources)

Fight Song (o) by Paul Tonner, arr. Gary Smith, p/c St. Joseph College

SAINT MARY-OF-THE-WOODS COLLEGE, Saint Mary-of-the-Woods

Saint Mary-of-the-Woods College Song (am) by Sister Gertrude '19 (w) and Dorthy Newland '32 (m), p/c Saint Mary-of-the-Woods College

SAINT MARY'S COLLEGE, Notre Dame

Praise and Honor (am) by Ann McCabe '56, p/c Saint Mary's College

The Bells of St. Mary's (o) (Tune, The Bells of St. Mary's, refer to Song Sources)

TAYLOR UNIVERSITY, Upland

Fight Song (fs) (Tune, Across the Field, refer to Song Sources)

UNIVERSITY OF EVANSVILLE, Evansville

College Hymn (am) by Wesley Shepard, p/c University of Evansville

Hail to Evansville (fs) by Wesley Shepard, p/c University of Evansville

UNIVERSITY OF NOTRE DAME, Notre Dame

Notre Dame, Our Mother (am) by Rev. Charles L. O'Donnell (w) and Joseph J. Casasanta (m), p/c Edwin H. Morris & Co.

The Notre Dame Victory March (fs) by John Shea (w) and Michael Shea (m), p/c Edwin H. Morris & Co.

Down the Line (o) by Vincent F. Fagan (w) and Joseph J. Casasanta (m), p/c Edwin H. Morris & Co.

Hike, Notre Dame (o) by Vincent F. Fagan (w) and Joseph J. Casasanta (m), p/c Edwin H. Morris & Co.

Notre Dame, We Hail Thee (o) by Daniel Pedtke, p/c not listed

Victory Clog (Damsha Bua) (o) by Robert O'Brien, p/c Oz Music Publishers

When Irish Backs Go Marching By (o) by Rev. Eugene Burke, C.S.C. (w) and Joseph J. Casasanta (m), p/c Edwin H. Morris & Co.

UNIVERSITY OF SOUTHERN INDIANA, Evansville

USI Varsity (am) by Joel Marsh (wa) (Tune, adapted from ISUE Varsity [1983]), p/c not listed

Sky On, Screaming Eagles (fs) by Tim Buescher, p/c not listed [1985]

VALPARAISO UNIVERSITY, Valparaiso

Hail to the Brown and Gold (am) (Tune, How Can I Leave Thee?, refer to Song Sources), lyrics attributed to various persons: Oscar C. Kreinheder (president of the university) and faculty member Margaret Ball Dickson (English Department); another source lists two members of the music faculty, Harold Rogers and Helen Dvorak, p/c Valparaiso University (c) [1935]

On to Victory (fs) by Margaret J. Marquart, Geneva G. Dye, and Edward A. Anderson (w), August Bucci (m), p/c not listed (c) [1930]

Hail Crusaders! (ofs) (Tune, On to Victory), new lyrics written under new title [1956]

IOWA

BRIAR CLIFF COLLEGE, Sioux City

The Briar Cliff College School Song (o) by Sister M. Arnold Staudt, arr. Lance Lehmberg, p/c Briar Cliff College

BUENA VISTA COLLEGE, Storm Lake

Buena Vista Alma Mater (am) (Tune, Amici, refer to Song Sources)

Buena Vista Fight Song (fs) by W. P. Green, p/c not listed

CENTRAL COLLEGE OF IOWA, Pella

Hymn to Central Youth (am) by Joyce Huibregise Kuyper, arr. Robert Rittenhouse, p/c Central College of Iowa

Go Central, Go (fs) by James Wilson, arr. Tom Cook, p/c Central College of Iowa

CCI (o) by George Cavanaugh, arr. Robert Rittenhouse, p/c Central College of Iowa

COE COLLEGE, Cedar Rapids

Coe Loyalty (am) by Risser Patty, p/c not listed

Coe Fight Song (fs) by Dan Calkins, p/c not listed

CORNELL COLLEGE, Mt. Vernon

Cornell, Greater Be Thy Name (am) by T. Stanley Skinner, p/c Horace Alden Miller

Cornell Fights (fs) by Claude E. Rose, p/c Cornell College

Fair, Old Cornell (o) by Horace Lozier, p/c Horace Lozier

DRAKE UNIVERSITY, Des Moines

Drake Alma Mater (am) by Clifford Bloom, p/c not listed

The D Song (fs) no w/m credit given, p/c not listed

EASTERN IOWA COMMUNITY COLLEGE DISTRICT, Clinton

Alma Mater (am) by Khwaja, p/c Eastern Iowa Community College

Clinton Jr. College Loyalty (fs) by C. Rydstrand, p/c Eastern Iowa Community College District, Clinton Campus

ELLSWORTH COMMUNITY COLLEGE, Iowa Falls

Fight Song (fs) (Tune, Washington and Lee Swing, refer to Song Sources)

GRACELAND COLLEGE, Lamoni

Alma Mater Hymn (am) by R. A. Cheville, arr. Verna Schaar, p/c Graceland College

Graceland Forever (fs) by W. K. McElwain, arr. Thelma Silsey, p/c Graceland College

Go Graceland (o) by Ken Cooper, p/c Graceland College

GRINNELL COLLEGE, Grinnell

Sons of Old Grinnell (am) by J. Norman Hall, p/c Grinnell College

Here Come the Pioneers (fs) by H. W. Matlack, p/c Grinnell College

Alumni Song (Iowa College) (o) by W. B. Olds, p/c Grinnell College

Come Ye Back to Old Grinnell (o) by W. B. Olds, p/c PD

Grinnell Doxology (o) by Pierce and Herrick, p/c Grinnell College

Grinnell Hymn (o) by Mabel Woodworth, p/c Grinnell College

IOWA LAKES COMMUNITY COLLEGE, Estherville

ILCC Fight Song (fs) by Mike Day, p/c Iowa Lake's Community College

IOWA STATE UNIVERSITY OF SCIENCE AND TECHNOLOGY, Ames

The Bells of Iowa State (am) by Jim Wilson, p/c Iowa State University

Iowa State Fights (fs) by Jack Parker, Manley Rice, and Paul Onam, arr. Rosalind K. Cook, p/c Howard Chase and O. L. Flaugher

Rise Sons of Iowa State (ofs) by Welch Richardson and Howard Chase, p/c Iowa State University

Alma Mater (o) (Tune, Amici, refer to Song Sources), J. C. Harris (wa), p/c Iowa State University

IOWA WESLEYAN COLLEGE, Mount Pleasant

Alma Mater (am) (Tune, O Tannenbaum, refer to Song Sources)

Fight Song (fs) (Tune, Washington and Lee Swing, refer to Song Sources)

Long May Our College Stand (o), no w/m credit given, p/c PD

IOWA WESTERN COMMUNITY COLLEGE, Council Bluffs

Hail to Iowa Western (am) by N. E. Crow, p/c Iowa Western Community College

LORAS COLLEGE, Dubuque

Fight Song (fs) (Tune, Hail to the Varsity, refer to Song Sources)

LUTHER COLLEGE, Decorah

To Luther (am) (Tune, There's Music in the Air, refer to Song Sources), G. B. Wollan (w), p/c PD

Luther Field Song (fs) by Arthur Tolo (w) and Norvald Mackestad (m), p/c Luther College

Luther Hymn (o) (Tune, Navy Hymn, refer to Song Sources), (wa) J. W. Ylvisaker, p/c not listed

MARSHALLTOWN COMMUNITY COLLEGE, IOWA VALLEY COMMUNITY COLLEGE DISTRICT, Marshalltown

Alma Mater (am) (Tune, Annie Lisle, refer to Song Sources)

Fight Song (fs) by Max S. Barker, p/c Bifco Press

MORNINGSIDE COLLEGE, Sioux City

Morningside Hymn (am) by James Wood, p/c Morningside College

Men of the M (fs), no w/m credit given, p/c Morningside College

MOUNT MERCY COLLEGE, Cedar Rapids

Mount Mercy Alma Mater (am) by Linda Williams, p/c Mount Mercy College Music Department (c) [1979]

NORTH IOWA AREA COMMUNITY COLLEGE, Mason City

Fight Song (fs) (Tune, Illinois Loyalty, refer to Song Sources)

NORTHWESTERN COLLEGE, Orange City

Northwestern Alma Mater (am) (Tune, Dutch National Anthem, refer to Song Sources)

Fight Song (fs) (Tune, Go U Northwestern, refer to Song Sources)

OTTUMWA HEIGHTS COLLEGE, Ottumwa

Alma Mater (am) (Tune, The Coronation March from "Le Prophete," refer to Song Sources), W. J. Kerrigan (wa), p/c Ottumwa Heights College

ST. AMBROSE UNIVERSITY, Davenport

Ambrosian Notes (am) (Tune, Finlandia, refer to Song Sources), W. J. Kerrigan (wa), p/c St. Ambrose University

Ambrose Fight Song (fs) by B. Schultz, p/c St. Ambrose University

SIMPSON COLLEGE, Indianola

The Red and Gold (o), no w/m credit given, p/c PD

SIOUX EMPIRE COLLEGE, Hawarden

Alma Mater (am) by Brown, p/c Sioux Empire College

Fight Song (fs) (Tune, On Wisconsin, refer to Song Sources)

UNIVERSITY OF DUBUQUE, Dubuque

Alma Mater (am) by Pernal, arr. James, p/c not listed

March on Spartans (fs), no w/m credit given, p/c not listed

UNIVERSITY OF IOWA, Iowa City

Alma Mater (am) (Tune, Believe Me If All Those Endearing Young Charms, refer to Song Sources)

On Iowa (fs) by W. R. Law, arr. Alford, p/c Edwin H. Morris & Co.

Iowa Fight Song (ofs) by Meredith Willson, arr. Oesterling, p/c Bourne Co.

Iowa Corn Song (o) by van Auken, p/c Hal Leonard Publishing Corp.

Iowa On to Victory (o) by Coulitti, arr. King, p/c State University of Iowa

Roll Along, Iowa (o) by Woodman, arr. Yoder, p/c Neil A. Kjos Music Company

UNIVERSITY OF NORTHERN IOWA, Cedar Falls

UNI Loyalty (fs), no w/m credit given, p/c not listed

UPPER IOWA UNIVERSITY, Fayette

Our College Home (o) by W. Ruggles, p/c PD

VENNARD COLLEGE, University Park

Hail, Vennard College! (am) by Kenneth Wells, p/c Vennard College

WALDORF COLLEGE, Forest City

All Hail to Thee, Oh Waldorf (am) by Alice J. Heilberg, p/c Waldorf College

Waldorf Fight Song (fs) (Tune, also known as College Song and/or Victory Song) by Ray Field, arr. Wilbur Anders, p/c Waldorf College

WARTBURG COLLEGE, Waverly

Fight Song (fs) by Bob Dotzauer, arr. E. Odegard, p/c Wartburg College

College of Our Bright Days (o) (Tune, Spanish Hymn from *Wartburg College Hymn Book,* also Christian Hymn refer to Song Sources), p/c Wartburg College

WESTMAR COLLEGE, Le Mars

O Westmar College (am) by Jewett, arr. Perrill, p/c not listed

Golden Eagle (fs) by Jewett, arr. Perrill, p/c not listed

WILLIAM PENN COLLEGE, Oskaloosa

Loudly Let Us Sing the Praises (am), no w/m credit given, p/c William Penn College

Fight Song (fs) (Tune, Notre Dame Victory March, refer to Song Sources)

KANSAS

BAKER UNIVERSITY, Baldwin City

Baker University Hymn (o) by J. Hatton, p/c PD

BARTON COUNTY COMMUNITY COLLEGE, Great Bend

Fight Song (fs) (Tune, Joyce's 71st N.Y. Regiment, refer to Song Sources)

School Song (o) (Tune, It's Great to Be a Trojan, refer to Song Sources)

BENEDICTINE COLLEGE, Atchison

To the Mount (am) by Sister Scholastica Kratschman, O.S.B., p/c not listed

Raven Song (fs) by Father Raphael O'Malley, O.S.B., p/c not listed

BETHANY COLLEGE, Lindsborg

Bethany College Alma Mater (am) by Lu Ruth Anderson (w) and Lloyd Spear and Ralph Harrel (m), p/c Bethany College

Bethany College Fight Song (fs) by James Wood, p/c Bethany College

Tiger Rag (o) (Tune, Tiger Rag, refer to Song Sources)

BETHEL COLLEGE, North Newton

Alma Mater (am), no w/m credit given, p/c not listed

Fight Song (fs) (Tune, On Wisconsin, refer to Song Sources)

EMPORIA STATE UNIVERSITY, Emporia

Hail Emporia (am) by William Rhoads, p/c Emporia State University

Emporia Fight (fs) by William Rhoads, p/c Emporia State University

Fanfare and Fight Song (o), no w/m credit given, p/c not listed

Long Live Stuart Hall (o), no w/m credit given, p/c PD

FORT HAYS STATE UNIVERSITY, Fort Hays

University Anthem (am), no w/m credit given, p/c not listed

FRIENDS UNIVERSITY, Wichita

Friends University Hymn (am), no w/m credit given, arr. McKenney, p/c Friends University

Falcons Fight (fs), no w/m credit given, arr. Perry, p/c Friends University

KANSAS STATE COLLEGE, Pittsburg

Gold and Crimson (am) by Markwood Holmes, arr. Richard Cook, p/c Kansas State College of Pittsburg

Pep Song (fs), no w/m credit given, arr. Charles Carter, p/c Kansas State College of Pittsburg

Gorilla March (o), no w/m credit given, arr. Charles Carter, p/c Kansas State College of Pittsburg

KANSAS STATE UNIVERSITY, Manhattan

Alma Mater (am) by H. W. Jones, p/c not listed

Wildcat Victory (fs) by Erickson, arr. Moffit, p/c Hal Leonard Publishing Co.

MID-AMERICA NAZARENE COLLEGE, Olathe

Alma Mater (am) by Richard Cantwell and Donald Metz, p/c Mid-America Nazarene College

Mid-America Nazarene College (fs), no w/m credit given, p/c Mid-America Nazarene College

PITTSBURG STATE UNIVERSITY, Pittsburg

My Alma Mater (am) by Eva Jessye, p/c not listed

On to Victory (fs) by Willanova Pratt Heinrich, p/c not listed

SAINT MARY COLLEGE, Leavenworth

Saint Mary (am) by N. De Rubertis, p/c Saint Mary College

ST. MARY OF THE PLAINS COLLEGE, Dodge City

Fight Song (fs) (Tune, When the Saints Go Marching In, refer to Song Sources)

SOUTHWESTERN COLLEGE, Winfield

Alma Mater (am) (Tune, Annie Lisle, refer to Song Sources)
Fight Song (fs) (Tune, On Wisconsin, refer to Song Sources)

STERLING COLLEGE, Sterling

Alma Mater (am) (Tune, Take Thou Our Minds, Dear Lord, by Calvin W. Laufer), p/c PD
Fight Song (fs) (Tune, Go U Northwestern, refer to Song Sources)
Hail to Sterling (o), no w/m credit given, p/c not listed

TABOR COLLEGE, Hillsboro

Alma Mater (am) (Tune, Annie Lisle, refer to Song Sources)
Fight Song (fs) (Tune, On Wisconsin, refer to Song Sources)

UNIVERSITY OF KANSAS, Lawrence

Crimson and Blue (am) by Bowles, arr. Gori, p/c Edwin H. Morris & Co.
Stand Up and Cheer (fs) by Bowles, arr. Gori, p/c Edwin H. Morris & Co.
I'm a Jayhawk (ofs) by Bowles, arr. Gori, p/c Edwin H. Morris & Co.
Three Cheers for KSU (ofs), no w/m credit given, p/c PD
Happy Jayhawk (Fighting Jayhawk) (o) by Bill Davis, p/c Edwin H. Morris & Co.

WASHBURN UNIVERSITY, Topeka

Alma Mater (am) by Frances Storrs Johnson and Lucy Platt Harsbarger, p/c not listed

For Washburn and Her Team (fs) (Tune, Ever True to Brown, as included in *Songs of Brown University,* Providence, RI), refer to Song Sources

WICHITA STATE UNIVERSITY, Wichita

WSU Alma Mater (am), no w/m credit given, arr. Boyd, p/c Wichita State University

Hail Wichita (fs), no w/m credit given, arr. Boyd, p/c Wichita State University

KENTUCKY

ALICE LLOYD COLLEGE, Pippa Passes

Alma Mater (am) (Tune, Annie Lisle, refer to Song Sources)

The Ballad of Alice Lloyd (o) (arranged for voices, SATB) by Abner Grender, p/c Pro Art Publications, Inc.

Deep Down in a Valley (o) by Abner Grender, p/c Alice Lloyd College

ASBURY COLLEGE, Wilmore

Asbury College March (am) by Irene M. Ihdre, p/c not listed

BELLARMINE COLLEGE, Louisville

Bellarmine Fight Song (fs) by Knoop, arr. Coin, p/c not listed

CENTRE COLLEGE, Danville

Centre Dear (am) by Richard Warner, p/c Centre College of Kentucky

EASTERN KENTUCKY UNIVERSITY, Richmond

Alma Mater (am) by Nancy Evans (w) and Jane Campbell (m), p/c Eastern Kentucky University

Yea Eastern (fs) by Mary Catherine Burns (w) and Helen Hull Lutes (m), p/c Eastern Kentucky University

Hail, Hail Eastern Maroons (ofs) by Frank Wilcox (w) and Henri Schnabl (m), p/c Eastern Kentucky University

MOREHEAD STATE UNIVERSITY, Morehead

MSU Alma Mater (am) by Elwood Kozee (w) and Betty Jo Whitt (m), p/c not listed

MSU Fight Song (fs), no w/m credit given, p/c not listed

MURRAY STATE UNIVERSITY, Murray

Alma Mater (am) (Tune, Annie Lisle, refer to Song Sources), p/c Austin (wa), arr. Shahan, p/c not listed

Fight Song (fs) by Johnson, arr. Shahan, p/c not listed

The Old Grey Mare (o) (Tune, The Old Grey Mare, refer to Song Sources), arr. Shahan, p/c not listed

NORTHERN KENTUCKY UNIVERSITY, Highland Heights

Northern Kentucky University Alma Mater (am), no w/m credit given, arr. Carolyn Z. Hagner and Philip J. Koplow, p/c not listed

Fight Song (fs), no w/m credit given, p/c not listed

TRANSYLVANIA UNIVERSITY, Lexington

Hail Transylvania (am) (Tune, 1812 Overture, refer to Song Sources)

TU Fight Song (fs) by Michael Swaffar, p/c not listed

UNION COLLEGE, Barbourville

Union College Alma Mater (am) (Tune, Annie Lisle, refer to Song Sources)

Union College Fight Song (fs), no w/m credit given, arr. Allan Green, p/c Union College in Kentucky

UNIVERSITY OF KENTUCKY, Lexington

University of Kentucky Alma Mater (am) by Josephine Funkhouser (w) and Carl A. Lampert (m), arr. W. Harry Clarke, p/c PD

On On, U of K (fs) by Carl A. Lampert (w/m), arr. W. Harry Clarke, p/c PD

UNIVERSITY OF LOUISVILLE, Louisville

UL Fight Song (fs) by R. B. Griffith, arr. Robert Griffith, p/c University of Louisville

WESTERN KENTUCKY UNIVERSITY, Bowling Green

College Heights (am) by Mary Frances Bradley, arr. David Livingston, p/c Western Kentucky University

Stand Up and Cheer (fs) (refer to Song Sources)

Go, Toppers (ofs) by Ed Knob, p/c not listed

LOUISIANA

GRAMBLING STATE UNIVERSITY, Grambling

Grambling (am) (Tune, O Tannenbaum, refer to Song Sources), R. W. E. Jones (wa), arr. Conrad Hutchinson, p/c not listed

Fight Song (fs) by William Wiley and Conrad Hutchinson, arr. Conrad Hutchinson, p/c Oz Music Publishers

Black and Gold March (o) by Conrad Hutchinson, p/c not listed

LOUISIANA COLLEGE, Pineville

LC Alma Mater (am) (Tune, Annie Lisle and Yale Boola, refer to Song Sources)

LC Fight Song (fs), no w/m credit given, p/c not listed

LOUISIANA STATE UNIVERSITY AND AGRICULTURAL AND MECHANICAL COLLEGE, Baton Rouge

Alma Mater (am) by Downey (w) and Funchess (m), p/c not listed

Fight for LSU (fs) by Carazo, p/c Thornton W. Allen

Hey Fightin' Tigers (ofs) by Gene Quaw (w), no (m) credit given, p/c not listed

LOUISIANA TECH UNIVERSITY, Ruston

Louisiana Tech Alma Mater (am) by Graham, p/c Graham

Go Bulldogs Go (fs) (Tune, Go Raiders, Go, refer to Song Sources)

Tech! Tech! Tech! (ofs) by James Smith, arr. J. H. Reynolds, p/c not listed

LOYOLA UNIVERSITY, New Orleans

Loyola Alma Mater (am), no w/m credit given, p/c not listed

Loyola Fight Song (fs) by Milo B. Williams, Raymond McNamara, and Charles C. Chapman, p/c George F. Briegel, Inc.

MCNEESE STATE UNIVERSITY, Lake Charles

MSU Alma Mater (am) by Gaburo, arr. K. Love, p/c McNeese University

Fight Song (fs) (Tune, Joli Blond, refer to Song Sources)

NORTHEAST LOUISIANA UNIVERSITY, Monroe

NLU Fite (fs) by Boyd and Heitken, arr. J. White, p/c Northeast Louisiana University

NORTHWESTERN STATE UNIVERSITY, Natchitoches

NSU Alma Mater (am) (Tune, Die Wacht am Rhein, refer to Song Sources)

NSU Fight Song (fs) (Tune, British Eighth March, refer to Song Sources), arr. Tom Wallace, p/c not listed

ST. MARY'S DOMINICAN COLLEGE, New Orleans

Veritas (am), no w/m credit given, p/c not listed

SOUTHERN UNIVERSITY AND A & M COLLEGE, Baton Rouge

Southern, Dear Southern (am) by Robert Brown, p/c not listed

Southern University Fight Song (fs) by Dr. Huel Perkins, p/c Oz Music Publishers

Southern University Pep Song (o) by Dr. Huel Perkins, p/c not listed

SOUTHEASTERN LOUISIANA UNIVERSITY, Hammond

Southeastern Alma Mater (am) by Ruth Smith, arr. Dr. Ralph Pottle, p/c Southeastern Louisiana University

Green and Gold Fight Song (fs) by James M. Stafford, arr. Grier Williams, p/c Southeastern Louisiana College

TULANE UNIVERSITY, New Orleans

TU Alma Mater (am) by Williams and Ruebush, p/c not listed

Roll On, Tulane (fs) by Tenhoor and Goldstein, p/c Thornton W. Allen

TU Fight Song (ofs) by Kline and Goldstein, p/c Associated Music Publishers, Inc. (Thornton W. Allen)

UNIVERSITY OF NEW ORLEANS, New Orleans

UNO, Our Alma Mater (am) (Tune, Consecration of the House Overture by Ludwig van Beethoven), Deborah H. Crosby (wa), p/c not listed

Let's Hear It for UNO (fs) by Lois D. Ostrolenk, p/c not listed

UNIVERSITY OF SOUTHWESTERN LOUISIANA, Lafayette

The University of Southwestern Louisiana Alma Mater (am) by Fournet, arr. Pickering, p/c not listed

Fight Song (fs) by La Bauve, arr. Pickering, p/c not listed

Ragin' Cajun Fight Song (ofs), no w/m credit given, p/c not listed

MAINE

BATES COLLEGE, Lewiston

Our Honored Bates (o), no w/m credit given, p/c PD

BOWDOIN COLLEGE, Brunswick

Bowdoin Beata (o), no w/m credit given, p/c PD

COLBY COLLEGE, Waterville

Mayflower Hill Song (am) by Ermanno Comparetti, p/c not listed

Hail, Colby, Hail (oam) (Tune, The Canadian National Anthem, refer to Song Sources), F. Lavaler (wa), p/c not listed

On to Victory (fs), no w/m credit given, p/c not listed

UNIVERSITY OF MAINE, Fort Kent

Alma Mater (am) by Boynton Fox, p/c Edwin H. Morris & Co.

UNIVERSITY OF MAINE, Orono

Stein Song (fs) and (am) by Lincoln Colcord (w) and E. A. Fenstad (m), arr. A. W. Sprague; rearranged Rudy Vallee, p/c Carl Fischer, Inc.

Fair Maine (ofs) by Bartlett, p/c not listed

O, Dear Loved Maine (o) by H. Estabrooke, p/c PD

MARYLAND

BOWIE STATE UNIVERSITY, Bowie

Bowie State University Alma Mater (am) by Charlotte B. Robinson, arr. Eugene T. Simpson, p/c Bowie State University

COPPIN STATE COLLEGE, Baltimore

Hail to Thee, Coppin! (am) by Miles W. Connor and Carloyd Thomas, p/c not listed

Fight Song (fs), no w/m credit given, p/c not listed

FROSTBURG STATE UNIVERSITY, Frostburg

FSU Alma Mater (am), no w/m credit given, arr. R. S. Binco, p/c not listed

Go Bobcats (fs) by Robert Cicco, arr. R. S. Bianco, p/c not listed

JOHNS HOPKINS UNIVERSITY, Baltimore

The Johns Hopkins Ode (am) by Wm. Levering Devries and Elizabeth E. Starr, arr. D. Coulter, p/c not listed

Veritas Vox Libereabit (am) (another title for the Johns Hopkins Ode listed above)

Rah! For the Black and Blue (o) by J. Girvin Peters, p/c PD

LOYOLA COLLEGE, Baltimore

Loyola Alma Mater (am) (Tune, Marcha de San Ignacio, *Province Newsletter,* Nov. 1977, p. 3) by Rev. William Davish, S.J. (w), arr. Betsie Devenney, p/c not listed

MONTGOMERY COLLEGE, Rockville

MC Fight Song (fs) by Dr. Ernest E. Wolfe, Jr., p/c Montgomery College

MORGAN STATE UNIVERSITY, Baltimore

Fair Morgan (am), no w/m credit given, p/c not listed

MOUNT SAINT MARY'S COLLEGE AND SEMINARY, Emmitsburg

Our Mountain Home (am) by Thomas B. Schmidt (w) and Rev. Joseph A. Schmidt (m), p/c Mount Saint Mary's College and Seminary

Fight, Fight for Mount Saint Mary's (fs) by Paul Wadde (w) and Rev. David W. Shaum (m), p/c Mount Saint Mary's College and Seminary

Hail, White and Blue (o) by Rev. Wm. McGonigle (w) and Rev. David W. Shaum (m), p/c Mount Saint Mary's College and Seminary

ST. JOHN'S COLLEGE, Annapolis

St. John's College March (am) by Adolph Torovsky, p/c not listed

ST. MARY'S COLLEGE OF MARYLAND, St. Mary's City

Alma Mater (am) (Tune, The Bells of St. Mary's, refer to Song Sources), Etta Costen Lochner (wa), p/c not listed

SALISBURY STATE UNIVERSITY, Salisbury

Salisbury State University Alma Mater (am), by Dr. Isabelle Thomas (w) and Margaret Black (m), arr. Dr. Arthur Delpaz, p/c not listed

TOWSON STATE UNIVERSITY, Baltimore

Alma Mater (am) (Tune, Abgenaki), no (w) credit given, George Coleman Gow (m), p/c not listed

Fight On (fs) (Tune, Bear Down, Arizona, refer to Song Sources), arr. Dana Rothlisberger, p/c not listed

UNITED STATES NAVAL ACADEMY, Annapolis

Navy Blue and Gold (am) by Joseph W. Crosley, p/c Edwin H. Morris & Co.

Anchors Aweigh (fs) by Lt. Charles A. Zimmerman, U.S.N., p/c Big 3 Music Corp.

Fight, Fight, Fight (Eyes of the Fleet, 2nd Verse) (o) by Rear Admiral J. V. McElduff, U.S.N., p/c Big 3 Music Corp.

The Goat Is Old and Gnarly (o) (Tune, Battle Hymn of the Republic, refer to Song Sources)

Navy Victory March (o) by Lt. W. Sima, U.S.N., p/c Big 3 Music Corp.

Salvo Song (Don't Give Up the Ship) (o) by Harry Warren, p/c Remick Music Corp.

UNIVERSITY OF MARYLAND, College Park

Hail! Alma Mater (am) by Robert Kenney, p/c Allen Intercollegiate Music, Inc.

Maryland Fight Song (fs) by Ralph Davis, p/c Allen Intercollegiate Music, Inc.

Victory Song (ofs) by Thornton W. Allen, p/c Allen Intercollegiate Music, Inc.

UNIVERSITY OF MARYLAND/EASTERN SHORE, Princess Ann

Alma Mater: University of Maryland, Eastern Shore (am) by Daniel Lyman Ridout, Sr., p/c University of Maryland, Eastern Shore

MASSACHUSETTS

AMHERST COLLEGE, Amherst

Alma Mater (am), no w/m credit given, p/c PD

Cheer for Old Amherst (o), no w/m credit given, p/c PD

Memory Song to Amherst (o), no w/m credit given, p/c PD

My College Days Must Have an End (o), no w/m credit given, p/c PD

ASSUMPTION COLLEGE, Worcester

Pledge We Our Loyalty (am) (Tune, Christe Sanctorum), Beverly Shaw Johnson (wa), refer to Song Sources [1985], p/c PD

BOSTON COLLEGE, Chestnut Hill

For Boston (fs) by T. J. Hurley, p/c Boston College Music Clubs

BOSTON UNIVERSITY, Boston

The Alma Mater (am) by Daniel L. Marsh, p/c not listed

Go, BU, Go BU (fs) by Randy Weeks, p/c not listed

BRADFORD COLLEGE, Bradford

To Bradford with Singing (am) by Carol Roy, p/c Bradford College

BRANDEIS UNIVERSITY, Waltham

To Thee, Alma Mater (am) (Tune, Academic Festival Overture, refer to Song Sources)

Brandeis Fight Song (fs), no w/m credit given, p/c not listed

The Blue and the White (o) by Irving Fine, p/c Irving Fine [1959]

CLARK UNIVERSITY, Worcester

Fiat Lux (am) by E. L. Clarke (w) and R. F. Fletcher (m), arr. Raffman, p/c Clark University

Sons of Clark (fs) by E. Leonard (w) and Charles Metcalf (m), arr. D.W.H., p/c Clark University

Clark Triumphant (o) by Zareh G. Thomajan, p/c Clark University

Fight (o), no w/m credit given, p/c not listed

COLLEGE OF OUR LADY OF THE ELMS, Chicopee

Green and Gold (am) by Sister Lawrence Marie, S.S.T., p/c not listed

Alma Mater (oam), no w/m credit given, p/c not listed

COLLEGE OF THE HOLY CROSS, Worcester

Alma Mater (am) (Tune, O Tannenbaum, refer to Song Sources)

Chu Chu (fs), no w/m credit given, p/c College of the Holy Cross

Crusaders March (o), no w/m credit given, p/c College of the Holy Cross

Fight! Crusaders (o), no w/m credit given, p/c College of the Holy Cross

Hoiah, Holy Cross (o), no w/m credit given, p/c College of the Holy Cross

Linden Lane (o), no w/m credit given, p/c College of the Holy Cross

EMERSON COLLEGE, Boston

O, Alma Mater Dear (am) (Tune, Old 124th), refer to Song Sources

Emerson, Our Emerson (o), no w/m credit given, p/c PD

FITCHBURG STATE COLLEGE, Fitchburg

In Old Wachusett's Shadow (am) by Priscilla Taylor, p/c not listed

FRAMINGHAM STATE COLLEGE, Framingham

Alma Mater Hymn (am) (Tune, Finlandia, refer to Song Sources), Martin F. O'Connor (wa), p/c not given

GORDON COLLEGE, Wenham

The Fighting Scotsmen (fs) (Tune, Scotland the Brave, also known as My Bonnie Lassie, refer to Song Sources), arr. Norman Richardson, p/c Hawkes and Son, Ltd.

HARVARD AND RADCLIFFE COLLEGES, Cambridge

Fair Harvard (am) by S. Gilman, p/c not listed

The Gridiron King (fs) by Richmond K. Fletcher, p/c Edwin H. Morris & Co.

10,000 Men (ofs) by Taylor and Anderson, p/c not listed

Harvardiana (o) by Williams, arr. Anderson, p/c not listed

Our Director March (o) (Tune, Our Director March, refer to Song Sources)

Soldiers Field (o) by Fletcher, arr. Anderson, p/c not listed

Veritas (o) by Fletcher, arr. Anderson, p/c not listed

Wintergreen (o) (Tune, Wintergreen for President, refer to Song Sources)

MASSACHUSETTS INSTITUTE OF TECHNOLOGY, Cambridge

Arise! All Ye of MIT (am) by Alvin Kuhn (w), no (m) credit given, p/c not listed

Technology (o) by Lloyd B. Haworth, p/c PD

MASSACHUSETTS STATE COLLEGE, Fitchburg

In Old Wachusett's Shadow (am) by Priscilla Taylor, p/c not listed

MERRIMACK COLLEGE, North Andover

Merrimack College Alma Mater (am) by Lawrence Farrell (w) and Rev. Thomas F. Walsh, O.S.A. (m), p/c not listed

MOUNT HOLYOKE COLLEGE, South Hadley

Alma Mater (am) by Gertrude Brady (w) and Gladys Pratt (m), p/c not listed

The Drinking Song (o), was used in the play *Uncommon Women and Others* by Wendy Wasserstein [1978], no w/m credit given, p/c *Mount Holyoke Songbook* (c) [1959]

Good Night (o) by M. P. Pingree, p/c PD

Holyoke (o), no w/m credit given, p/c PD

Groups wishing to obtain permission to perform these songs or to obtain the music for them should direct their requests to College Librarian, Williston Memorial Library, Mount Holyoke College, South Hadley, MA 01075.

Published Mount Holyoke College songbooks:

Mount Holyoke College. Class of 1899. *Songs of Mount Holyoke*. Boston: J. Frank Giles [1899]
Mount Holyoke College. Students League. *Mount Holyoke Songs*. South Hadley, MA: Mount Holyoke College [1906]
Mount Holyoke College. Le Giocose. *Songs of Mount Holyoke College*. Boston: C.F.W. Schlimper Music Press [1908]
Mount Holyoke College. Le Giocose. *Songs of Mount Holyoke College*. Boston: C.F.W. Music Press [1913]
Mount Holyoke College. Le Giocose. *Songs of Mount Holyoke College*. Boston: C.F.W. Music Press [1918]
Mount Holyoke College. Debating Society. *Songs of Mount Holyoke College*. Boston: Wm. F. Schlimper [1923]
Mount Holyoke College. Debating Council. *Songs of Mount Holyoke College*. Cincinnati: Otto Zimmerman & Son Co., Inc. [1928]

Mount Holyoke College. *Mount Holyoke Songbook.* Boston: Spaulding-Moss Co. [1959]

Copies of these books are out of print and no longer available for sale. Persons interested in obtaining a copy of any of these books should contact the Mount Holyoke College Library/Archives. South Hadley, MA 01075, which might have a duplicate copy to spare.

RADCLIFFE COLLEGE, Cambridge (Refer to Harvard College)

Radcliffe, Now We Rise to Greet Thee (am), by Floreta Elmore (w) and Emily Coolidge (m), p/c Boston Music Co. [1909].

There are three collections of Radcliffe college songs:

A Book of Radcliffe College Songs, p/c Boston Music Co. [1909]
Radcliffe College Songs, p/c Radcliffe Student Government Association, Cambridge [1923]
Radcliffe College Song Book, p/c not listed [1940] (photostat)

The above books can be photocopied (minimum order $5.00) by Radcliffe College Archives, 10 Garden Street, Cambridge, MA 02138

REGIS COLLEGE, Weston

High on the Hill Top (am) by S. M. Emmanuel, p/c not listed

SALEM STATE COLLEGE, Salem

Salem State College Alma Mater (am) by Hope Hilton, p/c not listed

School Song (fs) (Tune, The Orange and the Black, refer to Song Sources), p/c no credit given (wa) [1926–1927]

SMITH COLLEGE, Northampton

Oh Fairest Alma Mater (am) by Henry Sleeper, p/c Smith College

Fair Smith (o) by Blodgett, p/c Smith College

The Fair Transgressor (o) by Lillian Du Bois, p/c PD

S.C. Blues (o) by Lucinda Ross, p/c Smith College

The Stroke of the Sophomore Crew (o) by Alice Parker, p/c Smith College

SOUTHEASTERN MASSACHUSETTS UNIVERSITY, North Dartmouth

Alma Mater (am) by Barbara H. Noel, arr. Barbara H. Noel, p/c not listed (c) [1989]

SPRINGFIELD COLLEGE, Springfield

Now Raise a Song for Springfield (am) by Hyde-Vickers, p/c not listed

Show Me the Scotchman (fs) (Tune taken from the *Yale Song Book*), p/c not listed

TUFTS UNIVERSITY, Medford

Dear Alma Mater (am) by D. L. Maulsby (w) and L. R. Lewis (m), p/c not listed

Hymn to College Hill (o) by E. W. Newton, p/c PD

UNIVERSITY OF MASSACHUSETTS, Amherst

When Twilight Shadows Deepen (am) by B.I.N., p/c not listed

Fight Mass (fs) by B.I.N., p/c not listed

WELLESLEY COLLEGE, Wellesley

To Alma Mater (am) (Tune, The Mountain Maiden, no (m) credit given), Anne Barret Hughes (wa), arr. Flora Smeallie Ward, p/c Wellesley College

O Thou Tupelo! (o), no w/m credit given, p/c Wellesley College

WESTERN NEW ENGLAND COLLEGE, Springfield

WNEC Hymn (am) (Tune, Faith of Our Fathers, refer to Song Sources), B. A. Herman (wa), p/c not listed

WESTFIELD STATE COLLEGE, Westfield

Westfield, Alma Mater (am) by M. Ruth Reavey (w) and Louise Hagen Lane (m), p/c not listed

WHEELOCK COLLEGE, Boston

Wheelock College Alma Mater (am) by Judith Morse, p/c Wheelock College

WILLIAMS COLLEGE, Williamstown

The Mountains (am) by Washington Gladden, p/c Williams College

Yard by Yard (fs) by C. F. Brown, L. S. Potter, and H. B. Wood, p/c Williams College

'Neath the Shadow of the Hills (o) by T. M. Banks, p/c Williams College

Come Fill Your Glasses Up (o) (Tune, Corcoran Cadets March, refer to Song Sources), H. S. Patterson (wa), p/c not listed

WORCESTER POLYTECHNIC INSTITUTE, Worcester

Alma Mater WPI (am) by Willard Hedlund, p/c not listed

WORCESTER STATE COLLEGE, Worcester

Proud Lancers (fs) by Bernie Guarini, p/c not listed

MICHIGAN

ADRIAN COLLEGE, Adrian

Adrian Alma Mater (am) (Tune, Gott Mir Dir Mein Osterreich, refer to Song Sources)

AC Fite!! (fs) (Tune, Washington and Lee Swing, refer to Song Sources)

ALBION COLLEGE, Albion

Albion, Dear Albion (am) by Louis Rowland, p/c Albion College

ALMA COLLEGE, Alma

Alma College Alma Mater (am) by Samuel Jones, p/c not listed

Alma College Fight Song (fs) by Samuel Jones, p/c not listed

ANDREWS UNIVERSITY, Berrien Springs

Our Andrews U (am) by I. A. Steinel, revised Opal Young, arr. James Bingham, p/c Andrews University

AQUINAS COLLEGE, Grand Rapids

Fight On (fs) by Bruce Early, p/c Aquinas College

CALVIN COLLEGE, Grand Rapids

Calvin Alma Mater (am) (Tune, Calvinite March by Dale Grotenhuis), p/c Calvin College

Calvin Fight Song (fs) (Tune, Our Director March, refer to Song Sources)

Calvin Friendship Song (ofs), no w/m credit given, p/c Calvin College

Calvinite March (o) by Dale Grotenhuis, p/c Calvin College

CENTRAL MICHIGAN UNIVERSITY, Mt. Pleasant

Hear Us Now (am) by Ruth Mavis Williams, p/c not listed

The Fighting Chippewa (fs) by Loomis, arr. Dietz, p/c Neil A. Kjos Music Co.

CMU Fight Song (ofs), no w/m credit given, p/c not listed

Hail Chips (o) by N. C. Dietz, p/c not listed

C. S. MOTT COMMUNITY COLLEGE, Flint

C. S. Mott C. C. Alma Mater (am), no w/m credit given, p/c C. S. Mott Community College

C. S. Mott C.C. Pep Song (fs), no w/m credit given, p/c C. S. Mott Community College

Go You Bruins (o), no w/m credit given, p/c C. S. Mott Community College

EASTERN MICHIGAN UNIVERSITY, Ypsilanti

Our Pledge (am) by Edward Bowles, p/c not listed

Our Eastern Sacred Alma Mater (oam), no w/m credit given, p/c not listed

Huron's Fight Song (fs) by Lawrence Livingston, arr. Thomas Tyra, p/c not listed

FERRIS STATE UNIVERSITY, Big Rapids

Ferris Fidelity (am) by Graham T. Overgard, p/c Neil A. Kjos Music Co.

Fighting Bulldogs (fs) by Graham T. Overgard, p/c Neil A. Kjos Music Co.

GENERAL MOTORS INSTITUTE, Flint

Alma Mater: General Motors Institute (am) by R. J. Cleaton, arr. T. B. Martindale, p/c not listed

The Tech Song (fs) by Same Yance, p/c not listed

GRACE BIBLE COLLEGE, Grand Rapids

Stewards of the Mysteries (am) by Wayne A. Webb, p/c Grace Bible College

GBC Fight Song (fs) by Vernon Stromberg, p/c Grace Bible College

GRAND VALLEY STATE UNIVERSITY, Allendale

Hail to Thee, Grand Valley (am) by Arthur C. Hills, p/c not listed

Blaze Away (fs) (refer to Song Sources)

GVSU Victory (ofs) by Kathy Ure-Maris Tracy (w) and William Root (m), p/c not listed

HILLSDALE COLLEGE, Hillsdale

White and Blue (am) by Bess Hagerman, arr. R. B. Bowers, p/c Hillsdale College

Charge On (fs) by Jerry Bilik, p/c Hillsdale College

Hillsdale and the Blue (o) by Grace D. Moore, p/c PD

HOPE COLLEGE, Holland

Alma Mater Hymn (am) by Robert W. Cavanaugh, p/c not listed

Anchor of Hope (fs) by Morrette Rider, p/c not listed

Collegium (o) by Johannes B. Nykerk, p/c PD

KALAMAZOO COLLEGE, Kalamazoo

Kalamazoo College Alma Mater (am) by Willis Dunbar, arr. Lawrence Rackley, p/c Kalamazoo College

All Hail to Kazoo (fs) by Smith, arr. Lawrence Rackley, p/c Kalamazoo College

LAKE SUPERIOR STATE UNIVERSITY, Sault Ste. Marie

Laker Fight (fs) by Richard O'Briant, p/c Lake Superior State University

LAWRENCE TECHNOLOGICAL UNIVERSITY, Southfield

The LTU Hymn (am), no w/m credit given, p/c not listed

Dear Old LTU (fs) by H. O'Reilly Clint, p/c not listed

MADONNA COLLEGE, Livonia

Madonna College Song (am) by Sister Mary Francilene, SCCF, p/c Madonna College

MICHIGAN STATE UNIVERSITY, East Lansing

Michigan State University Shadows (am) by Traynor, arr. Leonard Falcone, p/c not listed

Michigan State Fight Song (fs) by Lankey, arr. Falcone, p/c Thornton W. Allen

MICHIGAN TECHNOLOGICAL UNIVERSITY, Houghton

Hail Alma Mater (am) by Paul Yoder, p/c Edwin H. Morris & Co.

Fight Tech Fight (fs), no w/m credit given, arr. Keranen, p/c Michigan Technological University

Copper County National Anthem (o) (Tune, Blue Skirt Waltz, refer to Song Sources)

NORTHERN MICHIGAN UNIVERSITY, Marquette

Hail, Northern (am) by West, arr. Richtmeyer, p/c not listed

Come Men of Northern (fs), no w/m credit, arr. Richtmeyer, p/c not listed

OLIVET COLLEGE, Olivet

Olivet Hymn (am) by York, p/c not listed

Olivet Victory Song (fs) by Hoekje and McCoy, p/c not listed

SAGINAW VALLEY STATE UNIVERSITY, University Center

Alma Mater (am), no w/m credit given, p/c not listed

Red and White (fs) by Dr. Charles Brown, p/c Saginaw Valley University

Cardinal Fight (ofs), no w/m credit given, p/c not listed

SCHOOLCRAFT COLLEGE, Livonia

Schoolcraft College Hymn (o) by Wayne Dunlap, p/c Schoolcraft College

UNIVERSITY OF DETROIT, Detroit

Victory of U of D (fs) by Don Large, p/c Plymouth Music

UNIVERSITY OF MICHIGAN, Ann Arbor

The Yellow and Blue (am) (Tune, Pirates Chorus by Balfe), Charles M. Galey (wa), p/c Edwin H. Morris & Co.

The Victors (fs) by Louis Elbel, p/c Edwin H. Morris & Co.

Varsity (ofs) by Earl V. Moore, p/c Edwin H. Morris & Co.

Ann Arbor University March (o) by G. D. Barnard, p/c PD

Rah! Rah! (o) by A. A. Stanley, p/c PD

WAYNE STATE UNIVERSITY, Detroit

Hymn to the University (am) by Vernon De Tar, p/c Louise W. Conklin

Hymn to Wayne (oam) by Nicholas Stanley Oates, p/c not listed

Tartar Men (fs) by Graham T. Overgard, p/c Belwin/Mills

Green and Gold (ofs) by Marian Morris, p/c Louise W. Conklin

War March of the Tartars (ofs) by Karl L. King, p/c Karl L. King Music House

Wayne University (ofs) by Fred Waring and Roy Ringwald, p/c Words and Music, Inc.

Win for Wayne (ofs) by Fred Busch and Fred Bergin, p/c not listed

WESTERN MICHIGAN UNIVERSITY, Kalamazoo

WMU Alma Mater (am) by Gilbert, p/c not listed

WMU Fight Song (fs) by Gilbert, p/c not listed

MINNESOTA

AUGSBURG COLLEGE, Minneapolis

Augie War Song (fs) no w/m credit given, p/c Augsburg College

BEMIDJI STATE UNIVERSITY, Bemidji

Bemidji University Hymn (am) by Joe Amato and Lance Davies, p/c not listed

Go Bemidji Beavers (fs) by Advanced Harmony Class of 1948, arr. E. O. Masoner, p/c not listed

BETHEL COLLEGE, Saint Paul

Alma Mater (am) by Whitiger, p/c not listed

Rouser (fs) by Leafblad, arr. Whitinger, p/c not listed

CARLETON COLLEGE, Northfield

Carleton Spelling Song (o) (Tune, Tramp! Tramp! Tramp!, refer to Song Sources), p/c PD

COLLEGE OF ST. CATHERINE, Saint Paul

CSC (am) by Sister Maris Stella, p/c Intercollegiate Music League

Hymn to St. Catherine (oam), no w/m credit given, p/c College of St. Catherine

COLLEGE OF ST. SCHOLASTICA, Duluth

Vivat (am) (Tune, On Wings of Song, refer to Song Sources)

COLLEGE OF SAINT TERESA, Winona

Our Fairest Alma Mater (am) by Lavinia Costello (w) and Helen Kirschstein (m), p/c College of Saint Teresa

COLLEGE OF ST. THOMAS, Saint Paul

Alma Mater (am) (Tune, Gaudeamus Igitur, refer to Song Sources)

Fight Song (fs) (Tune, When the Saints Go Marching In, refer to Song Sources)

CONCORDIA COLLEGE, Moorhead

Hymn to Concordia (am) by Herman W. Monson and Borghild Torvik, p/c Concordia College

Stand Up and Cheer (fs) by Herman W. Monson, p/c Concordia College

Concordia Forever (o) by Herman W. Monson, p/c Concordia College

CONCORDIA COLLEGE, Saint Paul

Fight Song (fs) (Tune, On Wisconsin, refer to Song Sources)

DR. MARTIN LUTHER COLLEGE, New Ulm

DMLC Alma Mater (am) by C. Trapp (w) and R. Shilling (m), p/c Dr. Martin Luther College

Hail, DMLC (fs) by Adolphe Wilbrecht, arr. Charles H. Luedtke, p/c Dr. Martin Luther College

FERGUS FALLS COMMUNITY COLLEGE, Fergus Falls

Fight Song (fs) (Tune, Washington and Lee Swing, refer to Song Sources)

GUSTAVUS ADOLPHUS COLLEGE, St. Peter

Alma Mater (am) by A. W. Anderson, p/c not listed

Fight Song (fs) (Tune, The Billboard March, refer to Song Sources)

HAMLINE UNIVERSITY, Saint Paul

Hail to Thy Colors (am) by Theodore Blegen, p/c not listed

Go, Hamline Go (fs) by Theodore Blegen, p/c not listed

HIBBING COMMUNITY COLLEGE, Hibbing

Hibbing Fight Song (fs) (Tune, The Victors, refer to Song Sources)

MACALESTER COLLEGE, Saint Paul

Dear Old Macalester (am) by B. B. Marvin, arr. B. B. Marvin, p/c not listed

Fight On, Macalester (fs), no w/m credit given, p/c not listed

MANKATO STATE UNIVERSITY, Mankato

Inaugural Hymn (am) by C. K. Waterman (w) and Paul Karvonen (m), p/c not listed

Mankato Rouser (fs) by Kenneth Pinckney, p/c not listed

MOORHEAD STATE UNIVERSITY, Moorhead

MSU Alma Mater (am), no w/m credit given, p/c not listed

Dragons' Golden Jubilee (trio only) (fs) by Arnold M. Christensen, p/c C. L. Barnhouse

NORTHLAND COMMUNITY COLLEGE, Thief River Falls

Fight Song (fs) (Tune, Fight On, refer to Song Sources)

RAINY RIVER COMMUNITY COLLEGE, International Falls

Rainy River Rouser (fs) (Tune, Wave the Flag, refer to Song Sources)

ROCHESTER COMMUNITY COLLEGE, Rochester

RCC Alma Mater (am) by Snesrud, p/c Rochester Community College

Fight Song (fs) (Tune, The Victors, refer to Song Sources)

ST. CLOUD STATE UNIVERSITY, St. Cloud

University Hymn (am) by Waughn and Dale, arr. Barrett, p/c not listed

SCSU Rouser (fs) (Tune, Down Main Street, refer to Song Sources), arr. Roger Barrett, p/c not listed

ST. JOHN'S UNIVERSITY, Collegeville

Alma Mater (am) by Rev. Innocent Gertken, O.S.B. and Rev. Dominic Keller, O.S.B., p/c St. John's University

Johnny Fight Song (fs) by Eugene Dupuch. arr. Rev. Innocent Gertken, O.S.B., p/c St. John's University

ST. OLAF COLLEGE, Northfield

The College on the Hill (o) (Tune, Auld Lang Syne, refer to Song Sources)

SOUTHWEST STATE UNIVERSITY, Marshall

Musical Cheers (fs) by William Moffit, p/c Hal Leonard Publishing Co.

The Horse (o) by Jesse James, arr. William Moffit, p/c Hal Leonard Publishing Co.

UNIVERSITY OF MINNESOTA, Crookston

Hail Minnesota (am) by Truman Rickard and Arthur Upson, arr. Ruth Heller and Oscar Duhle, p/c Edwin H. Morris & Co.

Minnesota Rouser (fs) by Floyd M. Hutsell, arr. Bencriscutto, p/c Edwin H. Morris & Co.

UNIVERSITY OF MINNESOTA, Minneapolis

Hail Minnesota (am) by Truman E. Rickard, arr. Bencriscutto, p/c Edwin H. Morris & Co.

Minnesota Rouser (fs) by Floyd M. Hutsell, arr. Bencriscutto, p/c Edwin H. Morris & Co.

Go! Gopher Victory! (o) (also known as The Gopher M), by Addison H. Douglas, p/c not listed

Minnesota Fight (o) by Truman E. Rickard, p/c Edwin H. Morris & Co.

Minnesota March (o) by Mike Jalma (w) and John Philip Sousa (m), p/c Sam Fox Publishing Co.

We Cheer for the U of M (o) by C. J. Zintheo, p/c PD

We're On Our Way (Rise Up and Shine) (o) by Frank J. Black, p/c not listed

WILLMAR COMMUNITY COLLEGE, Willmar

Willmar Fight Song (fs) (Tune, The Notre Dame Victory March, refer to Song Sources)

WINONA STATE UNIVERSITY, Winona

Hail! Winona (am) (Tune, Annie Lisle, refer to Song Sources)

WSC Rouser (fs), no w/m credit given, p/c not listed

MISSISSIPPI

DELTA STATE UNIVERSITY, Cleveland

DSU Alma Mater (am), no w/m credit given, p/c Delta State University

Drill Music for Patterns in Motion (fs) by William Moffit, p/c Hal Leonard Publishing Co.

EAST CENTRAL COMMUNITY COLLEGE, Decatur

ECCC Alma Mater (am) by Marguerite Dacy (w) and Elizabeth Bustin (m), p/c East Central Community College

East Central Community College Fight Song (fs) (Tune, On Wisconsin, refer to Song Sources)

EAST MISSISSIPPI COMMUNITY COLLEGE, Scooba

Alma Mater (am) (Tune, Austrian National Anthem, refer to Song Sources)

Fight Song (fs) (Tune, Washington and Lee Swing, refer to Song Sources)

HINDS COMMUNITY COLLEGE, Raymond

Hinds Community College Fight Song (fs) (Tune, Chester, refer to Song Sources), p/c arr. J. Manchester

JACKSON STATE UNIVERSITY, Jackson

Jackson Fair (am), no w/m credit given, p/c not listed

JONES COUNTY JUNIOR COLLEGE, Ellisville

JCJC Alma Mater (am), no w/m credit given, p/c Jones County Junior College

Fight Song (fs) (Tune, Arkansas Fight), no w/m credit given, p/c not listed

MISSISSIPPI COLLEGE, Clinton

Mississippi College (am) by Mackie, arr. Sclater, p/c Mississippi College

Oh, Fight (fs) by Compre, arr. Sclater, p/c Mississippi College

MISSISSIPPI DELTA COMMUNITY COLLEGE, Moorhead

Alma Mater (am) no w/m credit given, arr. Joe Abrams, p/c Mississippi Delta Community College

Red and Black Boys (fs), no w/m credit given, arr. Joe Abrams, p/c Mississippi Delta Community College

MISSISSIPPI STATE UNIVERSITY, State College

Maroon and White (am) by Wamsley, arr. Haney, p/c Mississippi State University

Hail State (fs) by J. B. Peavy, p/c Mississippi State University

MISSISSIPPI UNIVERSITY FOR WOMEN, Columbus

Serene as the Dawning (am) by Patricia Pascall Eccles (wa) (Tune from Symphony No. 1 by Johannes Brahms, arr. and adapted by Dr. William L. Graves), p/c Patricia Pascall Eccles (w) and Mississippi University for Women.

Hail to Thee (fs) (Tune, Spirit of Independence, refer to Song Sources), p/c words by a Committee from the Class of 1921 including Eola Williams, Jane Williams, Emma Ody Pohl, and Vachel Lindsey, Mississippi University for Women

[A very complete collection of the songs of Mississippi University for Women is found in *MUW Songs We Love*. This is a collection of forty-eight MUW college songs from 1886 to 1979. This attractive publication is no longer in print, and the few remaining copies are not available for purchase. However, inquiries about its contents should be made to Andi Simmons, MUW Public Relations Office.]

TOUGALOO COLLEGE, Tougaloo

Alma Mater (am) (Tune, Annie Lisle, refer to Song Sources), Jonathan Henderson Brooks (w), p/c not listed

UNIVERSITY OF MISSISSIPPI, Oxford

Alma Mater (am) (Tune, Annie Lisle, refer to Song Sources), no (wa) credit given, p/c not listed

Rebel March (fs) by Yerby, arr. Fox, p/c University of Mississippi

UNIVERSITY OF MISSISSIPPI, University

Alma Mater (am) by Mrs. A. W. Kahle (w) and W. F. Kahle (m), p/c not listed

UNIVERSITY OF SOUTHERN MISSISSIPPI, Hattiesburg

We Sing to Thee (am), no w/m credit given, p/c University of Southern Mississippi

Southern to the Top (fs) by Robert Hayes, p/c University of Southern Mississippi

WESTMINSTER COLLEGE, Florence

Westminster Chorus (am) by James Garrett, arr. J. W. Rawls, p/c Westminster College

WILLIAM CAREY COLLEGE, Hattiesburg

Carey College, We Will Love Thee (am) by Joan Geiger (w) and Dr. Robert L. Gauldin (m), arr. Dr. Robert Gauldin, p/c not listed [1962]

MISSOURI

CENTRAL METHODIST COLLEGE, Fayette

Here's to Thee (am) (Tune, Finlandia, refer to Song Sources)

Hail Victory (fs) by Robert Stepp, p/c Central Methodist College

Barnum and Bailey's Favorite (o) by Karl L. King, p/c C. L. Barnhouse

CENTRAL MISSOURI STATE UNIVERSITY, Warrensburg

Hail to Central State (am) by Carole G. Austin (w) and William Stoney (m), p/c Central Missouri State University

Go Mules (fs), no w/m credit given, arr. Holsinger and Coleman, p/c Central Missouri State University

CROWDER COLLEGE, Neosho

Crowder's Alma Mater (am) by Max Madrid, p/c Crowder College

Crowder's Fight Song (fs) by Max Madrid, arr. Bill Pierson, p/c Crowder College

DRURY COLLEGE, Springfield

Durry Alma Mater (am) (Tune, 1812 Overture, refer to Song Sources)

FONTBONNE COLLEGE, St. Louis

Fontbonne College Song (am) by Bezdek, p/c Fontbonne College

MISSOURI SOUTHERN STATE COLLEGE, Joplin

Alma Mater (am) by Mary Laird (w) and Emerson Jackson (m), p/c not listed

MISSOURI VALLEY COLLEGE, Marshall

Valley Will Shine Tonight (fs) (Tune, Our Boys Will Shine Tonight, refer to Song Sources)

MISSOURI WESTERN STATE COLLEGE, St. Joseph

MWSC Alma Mater (am) by Daryl McDermott (w) and Michael Matthews (m), p/c not listed

NORTHEAST MISSOURI STATE UNIVERSITY, Kirksville

Old Missou (am) by Basil Brewer, p/c not listed [1901]

NMSU Fight Song (fs) (Tune, Scotland the Brave, refer to Song Sources), arr. Norman Richardson, p/c Boosey Hawkes [1961]

NORTHWEST MISSOURI STATE UNIVERSITY, Maryville

Alma Mater (am) (Tune, Annie Lisle, refer to Song Sources)

ST. LOUIS UNIVERSITY, St. Louis

Varsity Song (am) by Alfred Robyn, p/c St. Louis University

Fight Song (fs) (Tune, When the Saints Go Marching In, refer to Song Sources)

SCHOOL OF THE OZARKS, Point Lookout

The School of the Ozarks Hymn (am) by Dr. John Mizell, arr. Leon C. Bradley, p/c not listed

Fight Song (fs) by Ron J. Johnson, arr. Alen Brackin, p/c not listed

SOUTHEAST MISSOURI STATE UNIVERSITY, Cape Girardeau

High Above the Mississippi (am) by Bera Beauchamp Foard and Wilhemina L. Vieh, p/c not listed

Fight Semo Fight (fs) by Le Roy F. Mason, p/c Oz Music Publishers

Go Eagles Go (o) by Le Roy F. Mason, p/c Oz Music Publishers

SOUTHWEST MISSOURI STATE UNIVERSITY, Springfield

Alma Mater (am), no w/m credit given, p/c not listed

UNIVERSITY OF MISSOURI, Columbia

Our Mizzou (am) (Tune, Annie Lisle, refer to Song Sources)

Fight Tiger (fs), no w/m credit given, p/c University of Missouri

Every True Son (o) (Tune, It's a Long, Long Way to Tipperary, refer to Song Sources)

UNIVERSITY OF MISSOURI, Kansas City

Alma Mater (am), no w/m credit given, p/c not listed

UNIVERSITY OF MISSOURI, Rolla

Alma Mater Hymn (am) by Nancy Cook Mackaman, arr. Joel I. Kramme, p/c University of Missouri-Rolla [1984]

Fight Miners (fs) by Harold W. Cleveland, arr. Harold W. Cleveland, p/c University of Missouri-Rolla [1984]

WASHINGTON UNIVERSITY, St. Louis

Alma Mater (am), no w/m credit given, p/c Washington University

Fight Song (fs), no w/m credit given, p/c Washington University

WEBSTER UNIVERSITY, St. Louis

There Is a University (am) by Inge d'Alquen Huber and Peggy Versen, p/c Webster University [1945]

Class Song (o), no w/m credit given, p/c not listed

Hail to Webster University (o), no w/m credit given, p/c not listed

Ivy Song (o), no w/m credit given, p/c not listed

Tassel Song (o) (Tune, Where, O Where Has My Little Dog Gone?, refer to Song Sources)

WENTWORTH MILITARY ACADEMY AND JUNIOR COLLEGE, Lexington

Wentworth (am) (Tune, Honey, Honey, Bless Your Heart), no w/m credit given, arr. Lewis, p/c Wentworth Military Academy and Junior College

Fight Away (fs), no w/m credit given, arr. Lewis, p/c Wentworth Military Academy and Junior College

WESTMINSTER COLLEGE, Fulton

Alma Mater (am) by John F. Cown (w) and Robert F. Karsch (m), p/c Westminster College

WILLIAM JEWELL COLLEGE, Liberty

Wm. Jewell Alma Mater (am), no w/m credit given, arr. Lakin, p/c William Jewell College

Western State Fight Song (fs) by Hawkins, p/c Neil A. Kjos Music Co.

Giant (o) by Tiomkin, arr. H. Conrade, plc. Witmark & Sons

MONTANA

COLLEGE OF GREAT FALLS, Great Falls

Ave Alma Mater (am) by N. Milton Iverson, arr. Wayne Peterson, p/c not listed

God of Our Fathers (oam) (refer to Song Sources), arr. Paul Lavalle, p/c Sam Fox Publications [1955]

Argo Fight Song (fs) (Tune, Aggie War Hymn, refer to Song Sources), no (wa) credit given, arr. Wayne Peterson, p/c not listed

MONTANA STATE UNIVERSITY, Bozeman

Fair MSU (am) by Mabel Kinney Hall, p/c not listed

Stand Up and Cheer (fs) by Edward A. Duddy and Paul P. McNeely (m), arr. Dr. Carl Lobitz, p/c Montana State University

NORTHERN MONTANA COLLEGE, Havre

NMC Hymn (am) by Hartwig, arr. York, p/c Northern Montana College

Go, Northern, Go (fs) by John Varnum, p/c Northern Montana College

Northern Lites (ofs) by John Varnum, p/c Northern Montana College

ROCKY MOUNTAIN COLLEGE, Billings

RMC Alma Mater (am) by Smith, arr. Knoll, p/c Rocky Mountain College

RMC Fight Song (fs) no w/m credit given, arr. Knoll, p/c Rocky Mountain College

UNIVERSITY OF MONTANA, Missoula

Up with Montana (fs), no w/m credit given, arr. Howell/Swingley, p/c University of Montana

WESTERN MONTANA COLLEGE OF THE UNIVERSITY OF MONTANA, Dillon

WMC, Here's to You (fs), no w/m credit given, p/c not listed

NEBRASKA

CHADRON STATE COLLEGE, Chadron

Alma Mater (am) by W. Boehle, p/c Chadron State College

Fight Song (fs) by R. Foster, p/c Chadron State College

CONCORDIA TEACHERS COLLEGE, Seward

Tower Song (am) by Dr. Th. Beck, p/c Concordia Teachers College

Concordia Fight Song (fs) by Ruth Petersen, p/c Concordia Teachers College

CREIGHTON UNIVERSITY, Omaha

The White and Blue (fs) by Gordon Raymond, p/c Creighton University

GRACE COLLEGE OF THE BIBLE, Omaha

Grace Bible Institute Hymn (am) (Tune, O God of Grace, by Franz Joseph Haydn), C. H. Suchan (wa), p/c Grace Bible Institute

Fight On to Victory (fs) by Dan Frizane, p/c Grace Bible Institute

HASTINGS COLLEGE, Hastings

Hastings to Thee (am) by Loren Ohlsen, p/c Hastings College

Broncos Fite (fs) by Loren Ohlsen, p/c Hastings College

KEARNEY STATE COLLEGE, Kearney

Kearney State Alma Mater (am), no w/m credit given, p/c not listed

KSC Fight Song (fs) by Lynn, arr. Crocker, p/c Kearney State College

NEBRASKA WESLEYAN UNIVERSITY, Lincoln

March of the Plainsmen (fs) by W. A. Fowler, p/c Nebraska Wesleyan University

The Yellow and Brown (o), no w/m credit given, p/c PD

UNION COLLEGE, Lincoln

Hail to Union College (am) by Robert Tan, p/c Union College

Slinga De Ink (fs), no w/m credit given, p/c Union College

We Pledge Our Lives in Service (o) by Perry Beach, p/c Union College

UNIVERSITY OF NEBRASKA, Lincoln

There Is No Place Like Nebraska (am) by Harry Pecha, p/c Edwin H. Morris & Co.

Dear Old Nebraska U (am) (same as above)

The Cornhusker (oam), no w/m credit given, arr. Nelson, p/c University of Nebraska

Hail Varsity (fs) by W. Joyce Ayers (w) and Chenowith (m), p/c Carl Fischer, Inc.

Hail Nebraska (ofs), no w/m credit given, arr. Nelson, p/c Nelson/University of Nebraska

March of the Cornhuskers (ofs) by Ribble, p/c Ribble/University of Nebraska

The Scarlet and Cream (o), no w/m credit given, p/c PD

UNIVERSITY OF NEBRASKA, Omaha

UNO Fite (fs) by James R. Sakee (w), no w/m credit given, p/c PD

WAYNE STATE COLLEGE, Wayne

Alma Mater (am) by Leon Berry, p/c Wayne State College

Fight Song (fs) (Tune, On Wisconsin, refer to Song Sources)

NEVADA

UNIVERSITY OF NEVADA, Las Vegas

The Mackay Song (am), no w/m credit given, p/c not listed

Win with the Rebels (fs) by Gerald Willis, arr. Gerald Willis, p/c PD

UNIVERSITY OF NEVADA, Reno

Hail Sturdy Men (fs), no w/m credit given, p/c not listed

NSU So Gay (o) by Lester R. Merrill, p/c PD

NEW HAMPSHIRE

DARTMOUTH COLLEGE, Hanover

Men of Dartmouth (am) by Richard Hovey (w) and Harry Wellman (m), p/c Dartmouth College

Dartmouth's in Town Again (fs) by Robert C. Hopkins, p/c Dartmouth College

An Atom (o) by A.D.E.W., p/c PD

As the Backs Go Tearing By (o) by Charles W. Doty, p/c Dartmouth College

Come Stand Up Men (o) by Moses C. Ewing, p/c Dartmouth College

Dear Old Dartmouth (o) by Walter Golde, p/c Dartmouth College

Glory to Dartmouth (o) (Tune, True Blue, refer to Song Sources)

KEENE STATE COLLEGE, Keene

Lift Voices High (am) by Katherine Day Bourne and Patricia Piper Bushey (w) and Ann Weeks (m), p/c Keene State College

PLYMOUTH STATE COLLEGE, Plymouth

Plymouth State College Alma Mater (am) by Anderson, p/c not listed

RIVIER COLLEGE, Nashua

Rivier! (o), no w/m credit given, p/c Sister St. Ida, Rivier College

SAINT ANSELM COLLEGE, Manchester

Anselmia (am) (Tune, O Tannenbaum, refer to Song Sources), no (wa) credit given, p/c not listed

UNIVERSITY OF NEW HAMPSHIRE, Durham

Alma Mater (am) (Tune, Lancashire, refer to Song Sources), H. F. Moore (wa), Henry Smart (m) [1898], p/c by the University of New Hampshire Bookstore, pub. E. C. Schirmer Music

New Hampshire Hymn (fs) by A. E. Richard, p/c not listed

On to Victory (The Line-Up) (ofs) by Florence V. Colege '12, arr. Larry Long, p/c (c) [1928] by the University of New Hampshire Bookstore, pub. E. C. Schirmer Music

Let's Give Three Cheers (o) [used for football] by "Knibbs" Fuller '06, p/c PD

Line'er Out for Old New Hampshire (o) [used for baseball] by A. E. Richards, p/c E. C. Schirmer Music

Refer to *University of NH Song Book,* p/c E. C. Schirmer Music

NEW JERSEY

BERGEN COMMUNITY COLLEGE, Paramus

Alma Mater (am) by Paul Marshall, Jr., p/c Bergen Community College

BLOOMFIELD COLLEGE, Bloomfield

Lux in Tenebris (am) by A. W. Fischer (w) and W. A. Berger (m), p/c Bloomfield College

CALDWELL COLLEGE, Caldwell

Beautiful Caldwell (am), no w/m credit given, p/c Caldwell College

COLLEGE OF SAINT ELIZABETH, Convent Station

School Song (o) by Elizabeth A. Loughlin Lortie (w) and Melba Knaus Loughlin (m), p/c College of Saint Elizabeth

FAIRLEIGH DICKINSON UNIVERSITY, Florham-Madison, Rutherford, and Teaneck-Hackensack

Alma Mater (am) by Goodhart-Davis, p/c not listed

JERSEY CITY STATE COLLEGE, Jersey City

Green and Gold (am) by A. Hayes, p/c Jersey City State College

Here Come the Gothics (fs) by J. Eversole, p/c Jersey City State College

KEAN COLLEGE, Union

Kean College, Alma Mater (am) by Lowell Zimmer (w) and Michael Montgomery (m), p/c not listed

MERCER COUNTY COMMUNITY COLLEGE, Trenton

Alma Mater (am) by Rosemarie Di Marino Flynn and William J. Flynn, p/c Mercer County Community College

MONMOUTH COLLEGE, West Long Branch

Alma Mater (am) by Tommy Tucker, p/c Tommy Tucker

Alma Mater (oam) by William A. Wollman (w) and Henry Smart (m), p/c not listed

Get Out and Go (fs) by Tommy Tucker, p/c Tommy Tucker

MONTCLAIR STATE COLLEGE, Upper Montclair

Montclair State College Alma Mater (am) by Evelyn Hock Walter '25, p/c not listed

NEWARK STATE COLLEGE, Union

Alma Mater of Newark State College (am) by Harry Robert Wilson (w) and Jack E. Platt (m), p/c Newark State College

NEW JERSEY INSTITUTE OF TECHNOLOGY, Newark

Alma Mater (am) by Frederick Fernsler (w) and James N. Wise (m), p/c not listed

PRINCETON UNIVERSITY, Princeton

Old Nassau (am) by Longlotz, p/c G. Schirmer, Inc.

Princeton Canon Song (fs) by Joseph Hewitt (w) and Arthur Osborn (m), p/c G. Schirmer, Inc.

Princeton Forward March (ofs) by K. Clark, p/c John Church Co.

Going Back to Nassau Hall (o) by K. Clark, p/c John Church Co.

The Orange and Black (o) (Tune, Sadie Ray, refer to Song Sources), Clarence B. Mitchell (wa), arr. Ernest Carter, p/c G. Schirmer, Inc. [1968]

Princeton Tigers (o) by E. H. Crane (w), no (m) credit given, p/c PD

Refer to *Collection/Carmina Princetonia,* songbook of Princeton University, p/c G. Schirmer, Inc.

RAMAPO COLLEGE OF NEW JERSEY, Mahwah

Ramapo, We Sing to You (am) by Michael Alasa (w) and David Welch (m), p/c not listed

RUTGERS UNIVERSITY COLLEGE, New Brunswick

On the Banks of Old Raritan (am) by Howard N. Fuller (w), no (m) credit given, p/c PD

Vive Les Rutgers' Sons (fs), no w/m credit given, p/c Rutgers University College

The Bells Must Ring (ofs) by R. M. Hadden, p/c Rutgers University College

Colonel Rutgers (ofs) by Kenneth M. Murchison, p/c J. Fischer and Bro.

Loyal Sons (o), no w/m credit given, p/c Rutgers University College

SAINT PETER'S COLLEGE, Jersey City

Hail, Alma Mater (am), no w/m credit given, p/c not listed

Fight Song (fs) (Tune, When the Saints Go Marching In, refer to Song Sources)

SETON HALL UNIVERSITY, South Orange

Alma Mater (am) by Byrne, arr. Montoni, p/c Seton Hall University

The White and Blue (fs) by Connor, p/c Seton Hall University

March "Setonia" (o) by Peach, arr. Medvec, p/c Seton Hall University

TRENTON STATE COLLEGE, Trenton

Blue and Gold (am) by Franklin Graper, arr. Helbig, p/c Trenton State College

Blue and Gold (fs) by John Kulpa, p/c Trenton State College

Victory March (ofs), no w/m credit given, p/c not listed

UPSALA COLLEGE, East Orange

Hail, Hail Upsala (o), no w/m credit given, p/c PD

WILLIAM PATERSON COLLEGE, Wayne

Alma Mater (am) by Prof. Mark Karp (w) and Earl Weidner (m), p/c William Paterson College of New Jersey

NEW MEXICO

EASTERN NEW MEXICO UNIVERSITY, Portales

Eastern New Mexico University Alma Mater (am) by A. Bruce Gardner, p/c not listed

Fight Song (fs) (Tune, Stars and Stripes Forever, refer to Song Sources), arr. Hank "Hound" Smith, p/c not listed

NEW MEXICO HIGHLANDS UNIVERSITY, Las Vegas

Cowboys (fs) by Mackey Joe Sulier, arr. Dr. Grady Green, p/c New Mexico Highland University

NEW MEXICO MILITARY INSTITUTE, Roswell

The Old Post (am) by Capt. Paul Horgan, p/c New Mexico Military Institute

NMMI March (fs) by Capt. F. E. Hunt, p/c Allen Intercollegiate Music

NEW MEXICO STATE UNIVERSITY, Las Cruces

Oh Didn't He Ramble (fs) (also, Aggies Fight Song), no w/m credit given, arr. R. Thielman, p/c New Mexico State University

Aggies Fight Song (fs) (same as above)

UNIVERSITY OF NEW MEXICO, Albuquerque

Alma Mater (am) by Lena C. Clawe, p/c University of New Mexico

Hail, New Mexico (fs) by Summer, p/c University of New Mexico

Fight On, Lobos (ofs) by Wm. E. Rhoads, p/c University of New Mexico

WESTERN NEW MEXICO UNIVERSITY, Silver City

Dear Alma Mater (am) by Capshaw, p/c Western New Mexico University

Rally Round You Mustangs (fs) by Weaver, p/c Western New Mexico University

NEW YORK

ADELPHI UNIVERSITY, Garden City

Alma Mater (am) by Magdalene Kurtz (w/m), p/c not listed [1921]

Adelphi University Fight Song (fs) by Patricia Wilson Sylvester (w) and Wilfred Roberts (m), p/c not listed [1966]

ADIRONDACK COMMUNITY COLLEGE, Glens Falls

ACC (am) by Frank Pryndl, p/c Adirondack Community College

NYSMTA March (fs) by Frank Pryndl, p/c Adirondack Community College

BERNARD M. BARUCH COLLEGE (CUNY), New York

Baruch Alma Mater (am) by Miriam Blech (w) and Rev. Grace Schulman (m), p/c not listed

BROOKLYN COLLEGE (CUNY), New York

Brooklyn College Alma Mater (am) by Robert Friend (w) and Sylvia Fine Kaye (m), p/c not listed

CANISIUS COLLEGE, Buffalo

Canisius College Song (am) (Tune, Canisius College March [trio]), Rev. J. G. Hacker, S.J. (w) and Carl Mischka (m), piano/vocal arr. Rev. James M. Demske, S.J., p/c Carl Mischka [1911]

Canisius College March (fs) by Carl Mischka, p/c Carl Mischka [1911]

CITY COLLEGE (CUNY), New York

Lavender, My Lavender (am) by Elias Lieberman and Daniel T. O'Connell (w) and Walter R. Johnson (m), p/c not listed

CCNY Fight Song (fs) by Fred Waring, Tom Waring, Pat Ballards, and Frank Hower

CLARKSON UNIVERSITY, Potsdam

Alma Mater (am), no w/m credit given, p/c not listed

COLGATE UNIVERSITY, Hamilton

Fight for the Team (fs) by Theodore W. Gibson, p/c Broadcast Music, Inc.

Colgate Marching Song (ofs) by F. M. Hubbard and G. M. Hubbard (Tune taken from Princeton Triangle Club Show, but title not given. This collection published by John Church Co. and the Princeton Triangle Club.)

Fight, Fight, Fight (ofs) by F. M. Hubbard (w) and R. L. Smith (m), p/c Broadcast Music, Inc.

In Eighteen Nineteen (ofs) by Robert G. Ingraham, p/c Broadcast Music, Inc.

Refer to *Songs of Colgate,* pub. 1958 by Broadcast Music, Inc. (in cooperation with the Colgate University Alumni Association)

COLUMBIA COLLEGE, COLUMBIA UNIVERSITY, New York

Sans Souci (am), no w/m credit given, p/c Alumni Federation of Columbia University

Stand Columbia (oam) (Tune, Deutschland Uber Alles, refer to Song Sources)

Roar Lion, Roar (fs) by Corey Ford, Roy Webb, and Morris Watkins, arr. George Briegel, p/c Allen Intercollegiate Music

Marching Song (ofs) by Charles H. Pattbery, p/c Alumni Federation of Columbia University

Stand Up and Cheer (ofs) (Tune, Stand Up and Cheer [University of Kansas], refer to Song Sources)

CONCORDIA COLLEGE, Bronxville

Alma Mater (am) by Robert "Buffalo Bob" Smith, p/c Concordia College

Hail to Thee, Concordia (fs) by Robert "Buffalo Bob" Smith, p/c Concordia College

CORNELL UNIVERSITY, Ithaca

Far Above Cayuga's Waters (am) (Tune, Annie Lisle, refer to Song Sources), p/c W. M. Smith and A. C. Weeks (w), p/c Edwin H. Morris and Co.

Give My Regards to Davy (fs), no w/m credit given, p/c not listed

The Big Red Team (o) by Charles Tourison, arr. J. S. Seredy, p/c Carl Fischer, Inc.

Carnelian and White (o) by Theodore Lindorff, arr. J. S. Seredy, p/c Carl Fischer, Inc.

Cornell Chimes/Evening Song (o), no w/m credit given, p/c Carl Fischer, Inc.

Cornell Victorious (o) by Hibbard Ayer, arr. J. S. Seredy, p/c Carl Fischer, Inc.

Fight for Cornell (o) by Theodore Lindorff, arr. J. S. Seredy, p/c Carl Fischer, Inc.

March On Cornell (o) by Marcel Sessler, arr. J. S. Seredy, p/c Carl Fischer, Inc.

ELMIRA COLLEGE, Elmira

All Sons and Daughters (am) by Mary Logan Bench, arr. Wing-Lester, p/c Elmira College

ERIE COMMUNITY COLLEGE (CITY CAMPUS), Buffalo

Hail to Thee (am) (Tune, Gaudeamus Igitur, refer to Song Sources), Constance Eve (wa), p/c Erie Community College, North Campus

Go, Kats! (fs) by Alan Raynor, arr. Alan Schmidt, p/c Erie Community College

FORDHAM UNIVERSITY, Bronx

Alma Mater Fordham, (am) by Rev. H. A. Gaynor, S.J. (w) and Frederic Joslyn (m), p/c not listed

Fordham Ram (fs) by J. Ignatius Coveney, p/c Fordham University

HARPUR COLLEGE OF STATE UNIVERSITY OF NEW YORK, Binghamton

Hail to Harpur (am) by J. Alex Gilfillan, p/c Harpur College

HERBERT H. LEHMAN COLLEGE (CUNY), Bronx

Alma Mater (am), no w/m credit given, p/c not listed

HOFSTRA UNIVERSITY, Hempstead

Prayer of Thanksgiving (am) by Kremser, arr. Von Rannon, p/c PD

March On, Hofstra (fs) by Wm. Kufe, p/c Wm. Kufe

HUNTER COLLEGE (CUNY), New York

The Good Ship Alma Mater (am) (no longer used) by Helen Gray Cone (w) and Prof. Mangold, p/c not listed

IONA COLLEGE, New Rochelle

Iona Alma Mater (am) by G. P. Lyons, p/c not listed

ITHACA COLLEGE, Ithaca

Ithaca Forever (am) by Alicia Carpenter (w) and Philip J. Lang (m), p/c not listed

LADYCLIFF COLLEGE, Highland

Alma Mater (am) by Sister M. Rosa, arr. Rybbka and Davis, p/c Ladycliff College

LONG ISLAND UNIVERSITY (Brooklyn Campus), Brooklyn

Alma Mater (am), no w/m credit given, p/c not listed

MANHATTAN COLLEGE, Riverdale

Alma Mater (am), no w/m credit given, p/c not listed

MANHATTAN (BOROUGH OF) COMMUNITY COLLEGE, New York

Alma Mater (am) by Dr. Ellsworth Janifer, p/c Manhattan Community College

MARYMOUNT COLLEGE, Tarrytown

The Blue of the Hudson (am), no w/m credit given, p/c Marymount College

MERCY COLLEGE, Dobbs Ferry

Alma Mater (am) (Tune, Concerto Grosso, Op. 6, No. 12 [slow movement] by Georg Frederick Handel), O. Sivack (wa), p/c arr. Dr. John Rayburn, Mercy College

NAZARETH COLLEGE, Rochester

Nazareth College of Rochester Alma Mater (am) by Sister Kathleen Reilly, S.S.J. (w/m), voice and keyboard arr. Sister Kathleen Reilly, S.S.J., wind ensemble arr. Dr. Albion Gruber [ca. 1975] and reharmonized and arranged for chorale [1985], p/c Nazareth College [c. 1940]

NEW YORK UNIVERSITY, New York

New York University Even-Song (am) by Duncan MacPherson '00 (w), p/c was published under the title "N.Y.U. Evening Song," words only (c) [1900]. It was published under the title "N.Y.U. Even-Song" [1901] arr. Cleveland Vernon Childs '00, p/c New York University. The "New York University Even-Song" was first formally referred to as "The Palisades," arr. Deems Taylor '06, p/c New York University. Current usage accepts the original song title "New York University Even-Song." When Genns wrote the alma mater in 1900, there was one undergraduate college at NYU (University Heights, Bronx). However, NYU had originated at Washington Square, where it continued to maintain several professional schools and an additional undergraduate college. Dorothy I. Pearce '48 wrote a verse that paid tribute to the Washington Square Campus. NYU closed the University Heights campus in 1973, and Washington Square again became the university's center. As a result, Pearce's verse is now more commonly used.

Old New York University (fs) by R. W. Ferns, '09 [Another Title, "The Fight Song," was listed in a 1968–1969 Student Handbook], p/c New York University

Fight for Your Violet (ofs), no w/m credit given, p/c New York University

Good-Bye (adversary's name inserted here) (ofs), no w/m credit given, p/c New York University

Good-Bye Rutgers (ofs), no w/m credit given, p/c New York University

The Girl of NYU (o) by Griffie Bonner '15 and Mike Halpern '14, p/c New York University

Here's to NYU (o), no w/m credit given, p/c New York University

The New Violet (o) by Willie Fletcher Johnson (w) and R. W. Atkinson (m) (Originally titled "Our Emblem," and the tune was "Aurelea," refer to Song Sources.) It is called "New Violet" to distinguish it from an earlier song called "The Violet," which has been changed to "The Old Violet."

All the above-mentioned songs were published in New York University songbooks, p/c New York University. The songs are not currently available on sale; they can be found in the University Archives. Please contact Teresa R. Taylor, Office of University Archives, Elmer Holmes Bobst Library, 70 Washington Square South, New York, NY 10012.

NIAGARA UNIVERSITY, Niagara University

Alma Mater (am), no w/m credit given, p/c not listed

Here's to Old Niagara (fs), no w/m credit given, p/c not listed

ORANGE COUNTY COMMUNITY COLLEGE, Middletown

Alma Mater (am) by Marvin K. Feman, p/c Orange County Community College

Men of Orange (fs) (Tune, March of the Men of Harlech, refer to Song Sources), Manuel Rosenblum (w), arr. Marvin K. Femen, p/c Orange County Community College

PACE UNIVERSITY, New York, Pleasantville, White Plains

Pace Alma Mater (am) by Evan Fox, p/c not listed

POLYTECHNIC UNIVERSITY, Brooklyn

Alma Mater (am) by Joan R. Bierly (w) and John La Barbara (w), p/c not listed

QUEENSBOROUGH COMMUNITY COLLEGE (CUNY), Bayside

Queensborough, Queensborough (am) by F. Kurzweil, arr. L. Pisciotta, p/c Queensborough Community College

RENSSELAER POLYTECHNIC INSTITUTE, Troy

Here's to Old RPI (am) by E. Fales, p/c not listed

Hail! Dear Old Rensselaer (fs) by Charles Root, arr. A. Olin Niles, p/c Rensselaer Polytechnic Institute

ROBERTS WESLEYAN COLLEGE, Rochester

Roberts Wesleyan College Alma Mater (am) (Tune, Chesbro Seminary Alma Mater), Mollie Staines (wa), arr. Ken Murley, p/c [ca. 1925] not listed

ROCHESTER INSTITUTE OF TECHNOLOGY, Rochester

Alma Mater (am), no w/m credit given, p/c not listed

Fight Song (fs), no w/m credit given , p/c not listed

ST. JOHN'S UNIVERSITY, Jamaica

Alma Mater (am) (Tune, O Tannenbaum, refer to Song Sources)

Red and White (fs) by Myers, arr. Phillips, p/c St. John's University

Redskin Ramble (o) by Harold Walters, p/c Rubank, Inc.

When the Saints Go Marching In (o) (Refer to Song Sources)

ST. LAWRENCE UNIVERSITY, Canton

Old St. Lawrence (am) by J. Kimball Gannon, p/c St. Lawrence University

The Scarlet and the Brown (fs) (Tune, The Mermaid, refer to Song Sources)

Against St. Lawrence Spirit (ofs) (Tune, Our Director March, refer to Song Sources)

Chapel Bells (o) by Eugene Wright, p/c St. Lawrence University

A Tribute (o) by John Brush (w) and Harry Shilkret (m), p/c, St. Lawrence University

STATE UNIVERSITY OF NEW YORK (SUNY), Fredonia

Alma Mater (am) by Shirley Hoeschele, arr. Ted Petersen p/c State University College

STATE UNIVERSITY OF NEW YORK (SUNY), Albany

College of the Empire State (am) by Francis Hubbard (w) and A. W. Lansing (m), p/c John Worley Co., (c) Ethel M. Houck [1917]; H. W. Gray Co. [1923] and [1929]

Alma Mater Beloved Dear College (oam) (Tune, Italia Beloved), Dr.

L. A. Blue (w), arr. Prof. Samuel Belding. This song was the original alma mater but was replaced by "College of the Empire State," which was written in [1916] and first published in [1917].

STATE UNIVERSITY OF NEW YORK COLLEGE, Brockport

Alma Mater (am), no w/m music credit given, p/c not listed

STATE UNIVERSITY OF NEW YORK COLLEGE, Buffalo

Our Finest Hour (am) by L. Harry Ray, p/c State University of New York College, Buffalo

Victory March (fs) by Robert Mols, p/c State University of New York at Buffalo

STATE UNIVERSITY OF NEW YORK, College of Agriculture & Technology, Cobleskill

Cobleskill Alma Mater (am) by Sheldon Guernsey, p/c State University of New York, Agricultural and Technical College

STATE UNIVERSITY OF NEW YORK COLLEGE, Cortland

Alma Mater (am) (Tune, The Hudson, NY High School Song [1914]), Ulysses F. Axtell (w), p/c not listed

STATE UNIVERSITY OF NEW YORK COLLEGE, Fredonia

Alma Mater (am), no w/m credit given, p/c not listed

STATE UNIVERSITY OF NEW YORK COLLEGE, Geneseo

Geneseo Alma Mater (am) by Ray Agnew, p/c Ray Agnew (c) [1981] used at such occasions as commencement.

Geneseo Alma Mater (oam) by Julia E. Silsby Twining (w) and Valma Horton (m), p/c not listed (c) [1925] used at events involving [pre-1981] alumni.

STATE UNIVERSITY OF NEW YORK COLLEGE, New Paltz

In a Valley Fair and Beautiful (am) (Tune, part of melody is from an Amherst College song, title not stated), Prof. Richards (wa) [1905], p/c PD

STATE UNIVERSITY OF NEW YORK COLLEGE, Stony Brook

Stony Brook Alma Mater (am) by Winston Clark (w) and Peter Winkler (m), p/c not listed

SYRACUSE UNIVERSITY, Syracuse

Alma Mater (am) by Junius W. Stevens, p/c not listed

Down, Down the Field (fs) by Lewis, arr. Goessling, p/c Syracuse University

UNION COLLEGE, Schenectady

Ode to Old Union (m) by F. H. Ludlow, p/c Graduate Council of Union College

Union's Game (fs) by Ed Moulton, p/c Union College

Come Now to the Campus (o) by C. E. Franklin, p/c Graduate Council of Union College

Dutchman's Song (o), no w/m credit given, p/c Graduate Council of Union College

If You Want to Go Union (o), no w/m credit given, p/c Graduate Council of Union College

Union Marching Song (o) by Homer Green and Jesse Winne, p/c Graduate Council of Union College

UNITED STATES MILITARY ACADEMY (ARMY), West Point

Alma Mater (am) (Tune, How Can I Leave Thee?, refer to Song Sources)

On Brave Old Army Team (fs) by Enger, p/c Shapiro, Bernstein & Co.

Army Blue (o) (Tune, Aura Lee, refer to Song Sources)

Benny Havens (o) (Tune, Wearing of the Green, refer to Song Sources)

Black, Gold and Grey (o), no w/m credit given, p/c PD

Fight Away (o) by F. Lehar, p/c PD

Gridiron Grenadier (o), no w/m credit given, p/c PD

Kings of the Highway (o), by General Burt, p/c PD

On to Victory (o), no w/m credit given, p/c PD

Slum and Gravy (o) (Tune, Song of the Vagabonds, refer to Song Sources)

UNIVERSITY OF ROCHESTER, Rochester

The Genesee (am) by T. T. Swinburne (w) and Herve D. Wilkins (m), p/c not listed

March, Men of Rochester (fs), no w/m credit given, arr. Frederick Fennell, p/c University of Rochester

VASSAR COLLEGE, Poughkeepsie

Hark, Alma Mater, Through the World Is Ringing (am) by Amy Wentworth Stone (w) and George Coleman Gow (m), p/c the Alumnae Association of Vassar College

Liberation Now (fs), no w/m credit given, p/c not listed

Ceremonial Music for Student Government Presidents (o) (Tune, Trumpet Fanfare from Act I, Scene I of "Simon Boccanegra" by Guisepe Verdi), p/c PD

NORTH CAROLINA

APPALACHIAN STATE UNIVERSITY, Boone

ASU Alma Mater (am), no w/m credit given, arr. Wm. Spencer, p/c Appalachian State University

Hi, Hi, Y-Ike Us (fs), no w/m credit given, arr. Wm Spencer, p/c Appalachian State University

ATLANTIC CHRISTIAN COLLEGE, Wilson

Alma Mater (am) (Tune, Russian Folk Song by A. Liadov, refer to Song Sources)

Pep Song (fs) by Harbaum, p/c Atlantic Christian College

BARBER-SCOTIA COLLEGE, Concord

The Barber-Scotia Alma Mater (am), no w/m credit given, p/c Barber-Scotia College

The Scotia Love Song (o), no w/m credit given, p/c Barber-Scotia College

BELMONT ABBEY COLLEGE, Belmont

Gather We from Far Flung Places (am) (Tune, Ode to Joy, refer to Song Sources), arr. Eugene Kusterer, p/c Belmont Abbey College

Hail to the Crimson, Hail to the White! (fs), no w/m credit given, p/c Belmont Abbey College

CATAWBA COLLEGE, Salisbury

Fair Catawba (am) by Bernice Keppel, arr. L. Bond, p/c Catawba College

The Victors (fs) (refer to Song Sources)

DAVIDSON COLLEGE, Davidson

All Hail! O Davidson! (am) G. M. Maxwell, arr. James C. Pfohl, p/c Thornton W. Allen Co.

O Davidson! (fs) by B. Ernest Shields, p/c Thornton W. Allen Co.

DUKE UNIVERSITY, Durham

Dear Old Duke (am) by R. H. James, p/c not listed

Blue and White Fighting Song (fs) by Leftwich, p/c Duke Musical Clubs

EAST CAROLINA UNIVERSITY, Greenville

Hail to Thy Name So Fair (am), no w/m credit given, p/c East Carolina University

EC Victory (fs), no w/m credit given, p/c East Carolina University

ELON COLLEGE, Elon College

Fight Song (fs) (Tune, Our Director March, refer to Song Sources)

FAYETTEVILLE STATE UNIVERSITY, Fayetteville

Alma Mater (am) by Mary T. Eldridge, p/c Fayetteville State University

Fight Song (fs) by Music Minors Class '66, p/c Fayetteville State University

GARDNER-WEBB COLLEGE, Boiling Springs

G-W College Alma Mater (am) by H. G. Hammett, arr. Jerry R. Hill, p/c Gardner-Webb College

G-W Fight Song (fs) by Jerry R. Hill, p/c Gardner-Webb College

GUILFORD COLLEGE, Greensboro

Alma Mater (am) by Scott, arr. Gansz, p/c Guilford College

HIGH POINT COLLEGE, High Point

In Praise of Alma Mater (am) by Lew Lewis, p/c High Point College

LENOIR-RHYNE COLLEGE, Hickory

Fair Star of Caroline (am) by John Seegers and Fred Smith, arr. Charles Carter, p/c Lenoir Rhyne College

LRC Fight Song (fs) (Tune, Illinois Loyalty, refer to Song Sources)

LIVINGSTONE COLLEGE, Salisbury

My Livingstone (am) by Fonvielle-Richardson, arr. J. E. Evans, p/c Livingstone College

The Black and the Blue (fs) by J. E. Evans, p/c Livingstone College

MEREDITH COLLEGE, Raleigh

Alma Mater (am) by Richard Tillman Vann, arr. Richard Tillman Vann, p/c not listed

METHODIST COLLEGE, Fayetteville

Hail to Thee, Our Alma Mater (am) by Lois Janet Lambie, p/c Methodist College

NORTH CAROLINA AGRICULTURAL AND TECHNICAL STATE UNIVERSITY, Greensboro

Dear A & T (am) by Dudley, arr. Carlson, p/c North Carolina Agricultural and Technical State University

NORTH CAROLINA STATE UNIVERSITY, Raleigh

NC State University Alma Mater (am) by Bonnie Norris and Alvin Foutain, arr. R. A. Barnes, p/c North Carolina State University

N.C. State Fight Song (fs) (Tune, United States Field Artillery March, refer to Song Sources)

The Red and White from State (o) by J. P. Watson, p/c North Carolina State University

PFEIFFER COLLEGE, Misenheimer

Hail, Pfeiffer College (am) by Dr. Richard Brewer, p/c Pfeiffer College

QUEENS COLLEGE, Charlotte

Queens College Hymn (am) by Moravian Bishop John Christian Bechler [1784–1857]), words by an advanced composition class taught by Prof. Laura Tillet [1956], p/c not listed

SAINT AUGUSTINE'S COLLEGE, Raleigh

Blue and White (am) by Wm. Augustine Perry, p/c Saint Augustine's College

SHAW UNIVERSITY, Raleigh

Hail, Dear Old Shaw U (am) (Tune, How Can I Leave Thee?, refer to Song Sources)

UNIVERSITY OF NORTH CAROLINA, Asheville

Alma Mater (am) by Dr. Frank Edwinn, p/c University of North Carolina at Asheville

Fight Song (fs) by Dr. Frank Edwinn, p/c University of North Carolina at Asheville

UNIVERSITY OF NORTH CAROLINA, Chapel Hill

Alma Mater (am) (Tune, Annie Lisle, refer to Song Sources)

Carolina Victory (fs) by McManeus, arr. Slocum, p/c University of North Carolina at Chapel Hill

UNIVERSITY OF NORTH CAROLINA, Greensboro

The University Song (am) by Laura Weill Cone (w) and W. A. White (m), arr. Belle Koravegay, p/c UNCG Alumni Office, Greensboro, NC 27412-5001

The Spartan Spirit (fs) by Dr. John Locke, p/c not listed

UNIVERSITY OF NORTH CAROLINA, Wilmington

Hail to Wilmington (am) by Charles Hunnicutt (w) and Lloyd Hudson (m), p/c University of North Carolina at Wilmington

Green and Gold (fs) by Dr. Graham Hatcher, arr. Jeff Lewis, p/c University of North Carolina at Wilmington [1990]

Sea Hawks Fight Song (ofs) by Bob Shaffer (w) and Carl Wilson (m), p/c University of North Carolina at Wilmington [1990]

WAKE FOREST UNIVERSITY, Winston-Salem

Dear Old Wake Forest (am) by Eatman-Paschal, arr. Huber, p/c Wake Forest University

Sing to Wake Forest (oam) by Huber, p/c Wake Forest University

Wake Forest Hymn (oam) by Helm-Sawyer, arr. Huber, p/c Wake Forest University

O Here's to Wake Forest (fs) by Weaver, arr. Huber, p/c Wake Forest University

Rah! Rah! Wake Forest (ofs) by Poteat, arr. Huber, p/c Wake Forest University

WESTERN CAROLINA UNIVERSITY, Cullowhee

Western Carolina University Alma Mater (am) (Tune, Annie Lisle, refer to Song Sources), William E. Bird (wa), arr. R. Trevarthen, p/c Western Carolina University

Western (fs) by Craddock and Tyra (w) and R. Trevarthen (m), p/c not listed

Fight On You Catamounts (fs) (same as above)

WINGATE COLLEGE, Wingate

Wingate College Alma Mater (am) (Tune, Annie Lisle, refer to Song Sources), p/c refer to *College Songs of N.C.*, edited by Hazelman-Brodt Music Co.

Wingate College Fight Song (fs) (Tune, On Wisconsin, refer to Song Sources), no (wa) credit given, p/c not listed

NORTH DAKOTA

DICKINSON STATE UNIVERSITY, Dickinson

DSC Fight Song (fs) by C. L. Woodward, p/c Dickinson State University

JAMESTOWN COLLEGE, Jamestown

Jamestown College Alma Mater (am) by Black, arr. Leo W. Froehlich, p/c Jamestown College

Jamestown College Fight Song (fs), no w/m credit given, arr. Leo W. Froehlich, p/c Jamestown College

MAYVILLE STATE UNIVERSITY, Mayville

Regent Square (am) by Henry Smart, p/c Mayville State University

Hail to Our Comets (fs) by Hans Lee, p/c Mayville State University

MINOT STATE UNIVERSITY, Minot

Beaver Fight Song (fs) by Ira Schwarz, p/c Minot State University

NORTH DAKOTA STATE UNIVERSITY, Fargo

Yellow and Green (am) by Dr. C. S. Putnam, p/c North Dakota State University

On, Bison (fs) by Ebling, arr. Putnam, p/c North Dakota State University

Fight Song (ofs) by Erickson, arr. Euren, p/c North Dakota State University

UNIVERSITY OF MARY, Bismarck

Mary University (am) by Robert E. Walter and Sarah Ann Walter, p/c University of Mary

Oh Marauders (fs) (Tune, Illinois Loyalty, refer to Song Sources)

UNIVERSITY OF NORTH DAKOTA (Lake Region), Devil's Lake

Fight Song (fs) (Tune, Go U Northwestern, refer to Song Sources)

UNIVERSITY OF NORTH DAKOTA, Grand Forks

Alma Mater (am) (Tune by Franz Joseph Haydn) by Roy La Meter and Norman Nelson (wa), University of North Dakota

Fight On Sioux (fs) by Raymond "Aimee" Johnson, p/c University of North Dakota

Stand Up and Cheer (ofs) by Raymond "Aimee" Johnson, adapted by Roy La Meter and Norman Nelson, p/c University of North Dakota

The Cannibal King (o), no w/m credit given, p/c University of North Dakota

It's For You—North Dakota U (o) by Franz Rickaby, p/c Franz Rickaby

VALLEY CITY STATE UNIVERSITY, Valley City

V.C.S.U. Alma Mater (am), no w/m credit given, p/c Valley City State University

V.C.S.U. Fight Song (fs), no w/m credit given, p/c Valley City State University

OHIO

ASHLAND UNIVERSITY, Ashland

Remember (am) by J. Ditmer, arr. Reeder, p/c not listed

Ashland University Battle Song (fs) by R. Thauvette, arr. Pachey, p/c not listed

On Eagles (o) by Rex Mitchell, p/c not listed

BALDWIN-WALLACE COLLEGE, Berea

BWC (am) by Arthur L. Breslich '98 (wa) (Tune from an old German drinking song), arr. Dr. Albert Rienemschneider '99, p/c Baldwin-Wallace College

Baldwin-Wallace, Hail Thy Name (oam) by Laurel Wagner Rittenhouse, p/c not listed

B. W. Battle Song (fs) by Katherine Olderman '28, p/c not listed

BLUFFTON COLLEGE, Bluffton

Alma Mater (am) by E. J. Hirschler (w) and Louella Geiger-Schmitt (m), p/c PD, out of print, copies in limited number available from Bluffton College

Hail to Ye College (fs) (Tune, Glorification March by George Rosenkrans, refer to Song Sources), Hilda Lette (w), arr. Helen Baker, p/c PD, out of print, copies in limited number available from Bluffton College

Alma Mater Pledge Song (o), Hilda Leete (wa), (Tune, Bring Home the Wagon, John, other titles are Oh Bring Home the Wagon, John, refer to Song Sources) p/c PD, out of print, copies in limited number available from Bluffton College

BOWLING GREEN STATE UNIVERSITY, Bowling Green

BGSU Alma Mater (am), no w/m credit given, arr. Louis Marini, p/c Bowling Green State University

Forward Falcons (fs), no w/m credit given, arr. Louis Marini, p/c Bowling Green State University

CAPITAL UNIVERSITY, Columbus

Alma Mater (am) (Tune, Finlandia, refer to Song Sources), arr. Barnhart, p/c Southern Music Co.

Pride of the Purple (fs) by Crist, arr. Barnhart, p/c Southern Music Co.

CASE WESTERN RESERVE UNIVERSITY, Cleveland

University Hymn (am) by Barbara Denison (w) and Petenpoll (m), arr. Wilson, p/c not listed

CWRU Fight Song (fs) by Robert Curnow, p/c not listed

Fight On, C.R. (o) by Anderson, arr. Curnow, p/c not listed

COLLEGE OF STEUBENVILLE, Steubenville

Hail! Steubenville (am) by Rev. Walter Plimmer (w) and Fred Waring (m), p/c College of Steubenville

The College of Steubenville Fight Song (fs), no w/m credit given, p/c College of Steubenville

Alumni Hymn (o) by J. P. Walter, arr. Alexander Schreiner as adapted from "Lorena" by J. P. Walter, p/c Carl Fischer, Inc.

DENISON UNIVERSITY, Granville

To Denison (am) (Tune, Oh Bring the Wagon Home, John, refer to Song Sources), p/c PD

Denison Marching Song (fs) by Gordon Lang (w) and Henry Arnold (m), p/c Denison University

War Cry (ofs) by Sara L. Howland, p/c Denison University

FRANCISCAN UNIVERSITY, Steubenville

College of Steubenville Alma Mater (am) by Father Walter Plimmer (w) and Fred Waring (m), dedicated to Father Daniel Egan [1950], p/c not listed. The alma mater is no longer used. The following song is used at graduation and other ceremonies:

Little Church Song (o) by Donovan, p/c not listed

HEIDELBERG COLLEGE, Tiffin

Sweet Alma Home (am) by F. A. Power, arr. Harry R. Wilson, p/c Heidelberg College Choir

Heidelberg Victory March (fs) by Myron Barnes, p/c Heidelberg College

HIRAM COLLEGE, Hiram

O Sons and Daughters (am) by Gladys Seymour Arnold, p/c Hiram College

Fight Song (fs), no w/m credit given, arr. Roger Topliff, p/c not listed

JOHN CARROLL UNIVERSITY, University Heights

Alma Mater (am) J. A. Kiefer (a/m), p/c not listed

Onward, On John Carroll (fs), no w/m credit given, p/c not listed

KENT STATE UNIVERSITY, Kent

Hail to Thee, Our Alma Mater (am) by Dwight Steere, arr. E. Turner Stump, p/c A Kent State University Publication

Fight On for KSU (fs) by Ed Siennicki, p/c A Kent State University Publication

KSU Victory March (o) by Douglass Chapman, arr. Ralph E. Hartzell, p/c A Kent State University Publication

MARIETTA COLLEGE, Marietta

Time Honored Marietta (am) (Tune, The Navy Blue and White, also Sadie Ray by J. Tannenbaum (c) [ca. 1870]), arr. James Bird, p/c White-Smith Publishing Co.

Fight Song (fs) (Tune, On Wisconsin, refer to Song Sources)

Marietta College Song (o) by Ralph Van Deman Magoffin (w) and Robert Spencer (m), p/c White-Smith Publishing Co.

O God, Our Help in Ages Past (o) (Tune, St. Anne, refer to Song Sources)

Old Marietta (o) (Tune, Die Wacht am Rhein [1854], refer to Song Sources), p/c Charles Gourlay Goodrich (w), PD

On the Banks of the Beautiful Ohio (o) by James Bird, p/c White-Smith Publishing Co.

Refer to *Songs of Marietta College* in Song Sources

MARY MANSE COLLEGE, Toledo

Alma Mater (am) by Joan Gradner, p/c Mary Manse College

Mary Manse School Song (fs) by Frederick Seymour, p/c Mary Manse College

MIAMI UNIVERSITY, Oxford

Old Miami (am) by A. H. Upham (w) and R. H. Burke (m), p/c not listed

Miami March Song (fs) by R. H. Burke, p/c not listed

MOUNT UNION COLLEGE, Alliance

Alma Mater (am) (Tune, Men of Harlech, refer to Song Sources), p/c arr. Whear, Mount Union College

On Mount to Victory! (fs) by Cecil Armitage, arr. Kandel, p/c Mount Union College

MUSKINGUM COLLEGE, New Concord

All Hail Muskingum (am), no w/m credit given, p/c not listed

Muskingum Fight Song (fs), no w/m credit given, p/c not listed

NOTRE DAME COLLEGE, Cleveland

All True Daughters of Our Lady (am) by Victoire and Gorman, p/c not listed

OBERLIN COLLEGE, Oberlin

Sing of Our Glorious Alma Mater (am) by Mrs. B. F. Stuart (w) and Louis Upton Rowland (m), p/c Oberlin College Alumni Association [1946]; reprinted with permission, Oberlin College Conservatory Library [1983]

A Song of Victory (fs) (Tune, Down the Street, refer to Song Sources), John Prindle Scott (wa), p/c Oberlin College Alumni Association [1946]; reprinted with permission, Oberlin College Conservatory Library [1983]

Also refer to *Songs of Oberlin* (Sesquicentennial Edition) in Song Sources. This is a facsimile reprint of the [1905] edition, with four favorite songs from later editions. It is edited and annotated by Carolyn Rabson and was published in [1983] by the Oberlin College Conservatory Library, Oberlin, Ohio 44074. The publication is available in paperback.

OHIO NORTHERN UNIVERSITY, Ada

ONU Hymn (am) by Bess L. Newton, p/c Bess L. Newton, published by the Alumni Association of Ohio Northern University

Sons of Old ONU (fs) by Frederick Thomas Kileen, p/c Frederick Thomas Kileen, published by the Alumni Association of Ohio Northern University

OHIO STATE UNIVERSITY, Columbus

Carmen Ohio (am) by Cornell, p/c Edwin H. Morris & Co.

Buckeye Battle Cry (fs) by Crumit, p/c Edwin H. Morris & Co

Across the Field (ofs) by W. A. Doughtery, Jr., p/c Edwin H. Morris & Co.

OHIO UNIVERSITY, Athens

Alma Mater, Ohio (am) by Kenneth S. Clark, arr. John Higgins, p/c Ohio University

Stand Up and Cheer (fs), no w/m credit given, arr. John Higgins, p/c Ohio University

Fight for Old OU (ofs) by William Brophy, p/c Ohio University

Go, Ohio (ofs) by Thornton W. Allen, arr. John Higgins, p/c Thornton W. Allen

OTTERBEIN COLLEGE, Westerville

The Love Song (am) by Grabill, arr. Huetteman, p/c not listed

The OC Fight Song (fs) by Grabill, arr. Huetteman, p/c not listed

UNIVERSITY OF AKRON, Akron

The University of Akron Alma Mater (am) (Tune, Annie Lisle, refer to Song Sources), arr. Jackoboice, p/c not listed

The University of Akron Blue and Gold (fs) by Fred Waring and Pat Ballard, arr. Jackoboice, p/c Words and Music, Inc. [1939]

Stand Up and Cheer (ofs), no w/m credit given, arr. Jackoboice, p/c not listed

Win for Akron (ofs) by Dilley, arr. Jackoboice, p/c not listed

UNIVERSITY OF CINCINNATI, Cincinnati

University of Cincinnati Alma Mater (am) by Otto Juettner (w/m), p/c University of Cincinnati

Cheer Cincinnati (fs), no w/m credit given, p/c University of Cincinnati [1927], renewed

Red and Black (ofs) by C. R. Beresford (w) and Alan T. Waterman (m), arr. A. T. Waterman, p/c University of Cincinnati [1927], renewed

Give a Cheer (ofs) by Jean Frances Small (w/m), p/c University of Cincinnati [1927], renewed

As the Backs Go Tearing By (ofs) (Tune, As the Backs Go Tearing By, refer to Song Sources)

UNIVERSITY OF DAYTON, Dayton

UD Anthem (am) by Dr. Maurice R. Reichard, p/c not listed

UD Victory (or U of D Athletic March) (fs) by Anthony McCarthy, p/c the University of Dayton Press

UD Loyalty March (or University of Dayton March) (o) by Louis Panella, p/c Frank A. Panella

UNIVERSITY OF FINDLAY, Findlay

Alma Mater Hymn (am) by John R. Van Nice, p/c not listed

Fight Song (fs) by Louis Chenette, p/c not listed

UNIVERSITY OF TOLEDO, Toledo

Fair Toledo (am), no w/m credit given, p/c not listed

U of Toledo (fs), no w/m credit given, arr. Jerry Bilik, p/c not listed

URSULINE COLLEGE, Pepper Pike

Ursuline College Song (am) by Sister Pauline, O.S.U. p/c not listed

WITTENBERG UNIVERSITY, Springfield

Wittenberg Alma Mater (am) by R. H. Hiller, arr. Ian Polster, p/c not listed

Wittenberg Fight Song (fs) by Ray Whitman, arr. Ian Polster, p/c not listed

WRIGHT STATE UNIVERSITY, Dayton

Wright State Alma Mater (am) by David Garrison (w) and Thomas Whissen (m), arr. William Steinhort, p/c Wright State University [1986]

XAVIER UNIVERSITY, Cincinnati

Dear Alma Mater, Xavier! (am), no w/m credit given, p/c not listed

Fight Song (fs), no w/m credit given, p/c not listed

YOUNGSTOWN STATE UNIVERSITY, Youngstown

Hail to Youngstown (am) (Tune, from Symphony No. 1 by Johannes Brahms), arr. Fleming, p/c not listed

YSU Fight Song (fs), no w/m credit given, arr. Fleming, p/c not listed

OKLAHOMA

CAMERON UNIVERSITY, Lawton

Cameron Pride (am) by Gene Smith, p/c Cameron University

Aggie's Fight (fs) by Gene Smith, p/c Cameron University

CENTRAL STATE UNIVERSITY, Edmond

Alma Mater (am), no w/m credit given, p/c not listed

Fight Song (fs) by J. J. "Pops" Gecks, p/c not listed

EAST CENTRAL UNIVERSITY, Ada

Amici (am) (refer to Song Sources)

Defenders of East Central (fs) (Tune, On the Mall, refer to Song Sources)

ECU Fight Song (ofs), no w/m credit given, p/c not listed

Fight On East Central (o), no w/m credit given, p/c not listed

NORTHEASTERN A & M COLLEGE, Miami

Hail to Thee, Northeastern (am) by faculty, p/c Northeastern A & M College

Fight Song (fs) (Tune, Go U Northwestern, refer to Song Sources)

NORTHEASTERN OKLAHOMA STATE UNIVERSITY, Tahlequah

The Northeastern State University Alma Mater (am) by Steve Wiles, p/c not listed

Northeastern (fs) by the student body, arr. Lehman, p/c not listed

Northeastern, Northeastern (ofs) by Henri Mensey, p/c not listed

NORTHWESTERN OKLAHOMA STATE UNIVERSITY, Alva

Northwestern Alma Mater (am) by Floyd McClain, arr. O. Stover, p/c Phi Beta Mu Fraternity

Ride, Rangers, Ride (fs) by Floyd McClain, arr. O. Stover p/c Phi Beta Mu Fraternity

OKLAHOMA BAPTIST UNIVERSITY, Shawnee

OBU, All Hail Thy Name (am) by Warren Angell, p/c Oklahoma Baptist University

Bison Rag (fs) by John Finley, p/c Oklahoma Baptist University

OKLAHOMA CHRISTIAN COLLEGE, Oklahoma City

Hail to Oklahoma Christian (o) by Harold Fletcher, p/c Oklahoma Christian College

OKLAHOMA CITY UNIVERSITY, Oklahoma City

Hail, Alma Mater (am) by James Morris, p/c PD

OCU—On to Victory (fs) by Keith R. Adams, p/c PD

OKLAHOMA STATE UNIVERSITY, Stillwater

OSU Alma Mater Hymn (am) by Robert McCullah, arr. Albert Lynd, p/c Oklahoma State University

Ride 'Em Cowboys (fs) by J. K. Long, p/c Oklahoma State University

ORAL ROBERTS UNIVERSITY, Tulsa

O-R-U (am), no w/m credit given, arr. A. Shellenbarger, p/c Oral Roberts University

O-R-U Victorious (fs) by L. Dalton, arr. B. Shellenbarger, p/c Oral Roberts University

PANHANDLE STATE UNIVERSITY, Goodwell

Crimson and Blue (am) by Milton Bradley, p/c not listed

Hail the Aggie Crew (fs) no w/m credit given, p/c not listed

PHILLIPS UNIVERSITY, Enid

PU Alma Mater (am) by Elizabeth Cleaver Bickford, p/c Phillips University

PU Chant and Victory March (fs) by Max Tromblee, p/c Phillips University (Refer to On Parade in Song Sources)

SOUTHEASTERN OKLAHOMA STATE UNIVERSITY, Durant

SSU Alma Mater (am) by Helen Edwards, p/c PD

Southeastern (fs) by Julia Munson (w) and Julia E. Stout and Pearl Shull (m), p/c PD

Hymn to the Blue and Gold (o) by Walter Britt, p/c PD

SOUTHWESTERN OKLAHOMA STATE UNIVERSITY, Weatherford

Alma Mater (am) by Mabry, p/c Southwestern Oklahoma State University

Stand Up and Cheer (fs), no w/m credit given, arr. Dick Coy, p/c not listed

UNIVERSITY OF OKLAHOMA, Norman

OU Chant (am) by Gilkey, arr. Clarkson, p/c University of Oklahoma

Boomer Sooner (fs) (Tune, Yale Boola, refer to Song Sources), p/c (w) University of Oklahoma

Oklahoma! (o) by Richard Rodgers, arr. John Cacavas, p/c Williamson Music, Inc. (Refer to Song Sources)

OK Oklahoma (o) by Fred Waring, p/c University of Oklahoma

UNIVERSITY OF TULSA, Tulsa

Hail to Tulsa U. (am), no w/m credit given, p/c not listed

Alma Mater (oam) by Crossman, p/c Crossman

Hurricane Spirit Song (fs) by Henneke, p/c Thornton W. Allen (Associated Music Publishers, Inc.)

OREGON

EASTERN OREGON STATE COLLEGE, La Grande

Hail Alma Mater (am) by L. R. Lewis p/c Eastern Oregon State College

Alma Mater (oam) by Iola Gooding Guard, p/c Eastern Oregon State College

Fight Song (fs) by D. W. Hall, arr. Ehlers, p/c Eastern Oregon State College

College Days (o), no w/m credit given, p/c Eastern Oregon State College

East Oregon (o) by Gene Schultz, p/c Eastern Oregon State College

Hail to Oregon (o) by C. H. Cleaver, p/c Eastern Oregon State College

Oregon State Song (o) by Henry Murtagh, arr. Daniel H. Wilson, p/c Eastern Oregon State College

Pioneer Song (o) (Tune, Finlandia, refer to Song Sources), p/c (wa) Eastern Oregon State College

Queen of the Mountain (o), no w/m credit given, p/c Eastern Oregon State College

Varsity (o) by Dr. Henry Ehlers, p/c Eastern Oregon State College

GEORGE FOX COLLEGE, Newberg

Close Beside Chehaleius' Mountain (am) by Pemberton and Hoskins (w) and Clifford Kantner (m), p/c George Fox College

MARYLHURST COLLEGE FOR LIFELONG LEARNING, Marylhurst

Marylhurst, Our Hearts Acclaim Thee (am), no w/m credit given, p/c not listed

NORTHWEST CHRISTIAN COLLEGE, Eugene

All Hail to Thee, Dear NCC (am), no w/m credit given, p/c Northwest Christian College

OREGON COLLEGE OF EDUCATION, Monmouth

OCE Hymn (am) by Perry B. Arant, p/c Oregon College of Education

OCE Fight Song (fs) by Cary W. Buchanan, p/c Oregon College of Education

OREGON STATE UNIVERSITY, Corvallis

OSU Alma Mater (am) by Homer Maris, p/c not listed

OSU Fight Song (fs) by Harold A. Wilkins, p/c not listed

PACIFIC UNIVERSITY, Forest Grove

Hail, Old Pacific, Hail (am) (Tune, Marche Slav, refer to Song Sources), arr. David Greenfield, p/c not listed

Pacific University Fight Song (fs) by Richard Greenfield, p/c Pacific University

PORTLAND STATE UNIVERSITY, Portland

Portland State University Fight Song (fs) (Tune, Men of Ohio, refer to Song Sources)

SOUTHERN OREGON STATE COLLEGE, Ashland

SOC Alma Mater (am) by Ray Tumbleson, p/c Southern Oregon College

SOC Fight Song (fs) by Mahlon Merrick, p/c Southern Oregon College

SOUTHWESTERN OREGON COMMUNITY COLLEGE, Coos Bay

There Will Never Be Another U (am), no w/m credit given, p/c Southwestern Oregon Community College

Knock the Jocks (fs), no w/m credit given, p/c Southwestern Oregon Community College

UNIVERSITY OF OREGON, Eugene

The Pledge Song (am) by John Stark Evans, p/c John Stark Evans

Mighty Oregon (fs) by De Witt Gilbert (w) and Albert Perfect (m), p/c Edwin H. Morris & Co.

Down the Field (ofs) (Tune, Down the Field, refer to Song Sources)

UNIVERSITY OF PORTLAND, Portland

University of Portland Alma Mater (am) by Margaret Vance, arr. Margaret Vance, p/c University of Portland [1975]

Portland University Victory March (fs) by John Lemmer and Rev. George L. Dum, C.S.C. (w) and Earl Clark and Rev. George L. Dum, C.S.C. (m) arr. Rev. George L. Dum, C.S.C., p/c University of Portland

On Pilots On (o) by Rev. G. L. Dum, C.S.C. p/c University of Portland

Prior to [1935] the University of Portland was known as Columbia University. *College Songs,* published by the Associated Oil Company prior to [1935], included the following songs:

Victory Team (fs), no w/m credit given, p/c not listed

Columbia's Fighting Team (ofs), no w/m credit given, p/c not listed

WILLAMETTE UNIVERSITY, Salem

Ode to Willamette (am) by F. S. Mendenhall, arr. M. W. Brennen, p/c Willamette University

Fight, Bearcats (fs) by Clara Wright, arr. M. W. Brennen, p/c Willamette University

PENNSYLVANIA

ALBRIGHT COLLEGE, Reading

Alma Mater (am) by Hans Nix, p/c Albright College

Albright Fight Song (fs) by Kenneth Kostenbador, p/c Albright College

ALLEGHENY COLLEGE, Meadville

Alma Mater Beatissima (am) (Tune, God of Our Fathers, refer to Song Sources), John D. Hammond (wa) and George W. Warren (ma), arr. Morten J. Luvaas [8 pt. choral arr., a cappella], p/c estate of Morten J. Luvaas, c/o Diane Le Rohl, 25585 Birch Bluff Road, Excelsior, MN 55331

BLOOMSBURG UNIVERSITY OF PENNSYLVANIA, Bloomsburg

Alma Mater (am) (Tune, Annie Lisle, refer to Song Sources)

Old Bloomsburg (fs) by Howard F. Fenstermacher, p/c Bloomsburg University of Pennsylvania

Hail to the Huskies (ofs) (Tune, Down, Down to Washington), no w/m credit given, p/c not listed

Across the Field (ofs) (Refer to Song Sources)

BRYN MAWR COLLEGE, Bryn Mawr

Bryn Mawr College Hymn (am) by Richmond Lattimor, translator of Greek/Latin text, no w/m credit given, p/c not listed

BUCKNELL UNIVERSITY, Lewisburg

Dear Bucknell (am) by S. S. Merriman, p/c Bucknell University

Alma Mater, Thee We Honor (oam) by Norman H. Stewart (w) and Paul G. Stolz (m), p/c Bucknell University

Go! Bisons (fs) by Campbell Rutledge, arr. M. Le Mon, p/c Bucknell University

Come Bucknell Warriors (o), no w/m credit given, arr. M. Le Mon, p/c Bucknell University

Hail, Bucknell (o) by W. C. Bartol (w) and P. G. Stolz (m), p/c Bucknell University

Hail! Hail! Hail! Bucknell (o) by H. M. Lowry, p/c Bucknell University

Ray! Bucknell (o), no w/m credit given, arr. M. Le Mon, p/c Bucknell University

CALIFORNIA UNIVERSITY OF PENNSYLVANIA, California

Alma Mater (am) by Phillip Rossi, p/c not listed

CARNEGIE MELLON UNIVERSITY, Pittsburgh

Alma Mater (am) by Prof. Charles Jay Taylor, p/c not listed

Fight for the Glory of Carnegie (fs) by Robert Schmertl, p/c not listed

CLARION UNIVERSITY OF PENNSYLVANIA, Clarion

Oh, Clarion, Dear Clarion (am) by Gladys Rich Michalski, arr. Stanley F. Michalski, p/c Clarion University of Pennsylvania

Carry On for Clarion (fs) by Paul Yoder, p/c Clarion University of Pennsylvania

COLLEGE MISERICORDIA, Dallas

Misericordia (am) by Sister Teresa Mary Moyles, p/c College Misericordia

COMMUNITY COLLEGE OF ALLEGHENY COUNTY, Allegheny Campus, Pittsburgh

Alma Mater (am) no w/m credit given, p/c not listed

Fight Song (fs) no w/m credit given, p/c not listed

DREXEL UNIVERSITY, Philadelphia

Drexel Ode (am) by James Dickinson, p/c Drexel University

Drexel Fight Song (fs) by T. Groo and G. Piercy, arr. C. Shive, p/c Drexel University

DUQUESNE UNIVERSITY, Pittsburgh

Duquesne University Alma Mater (am), no w/m credit given, arr. Joseph Willcox Jenkins, p/c Duquesne University

Alma Mater (oam) by John Mallory, C.S.Sp., p/c not listed

Duquesne Victory Song (fs) (Tune, from "Victory Portraits" by Sammy Nestico, p/c Volkwein Bros.)

The Fight Song (ofs) by Thomas J. Quigley, arr. Henning, p/c Volwein Bros.

EAST STROUDSBURG UNIVERSITY OF PENNSYLVANIA,
East Stroudsburg

Alma Mater (am) (Tune, Believe Me If All Those Endearing Young Charms, refer to Song Sources)

Hail, Dear Old Stroudsburg (fs), no w/m credit given, p/c not listed

EDINBORO UNIVERSITY OF PENNSYLVANIA, Edinboro

Hail to Thee (am), no w/m credit given, p/c not listed

Fight Song (fs) (Tune, Scotland the Brave, refer to Song Sources)

ELIZABETHTOWN COLLEGE, Elizabethtown

Alma Mater (am) by J. Via, p/c Elizabethtown College

FRANKLIN AND MARSHALL COLLEGE, Lancaster

Franklin and Marshall College Alma Mater (am) by John P. Alexander, p/c Franklin and Marshall College

Fight Song (fs) (Tune, Down the Field, refer to Song Sources)

GENEVA COLLEGE, Beaver Falls

Campus Song (am) (Tune, Ode to Old Union, refer to Union College, Schenectady, NY)

Hail, Hail Geneva (fs) (Tune, Down the Field, refer to Song Sources)

Moon on the Campus (o) by F. Filipone, p/c Geneva College

GETTYSBURG COLLEGE, Gettysburg

Alma Mater (am) by Paul S. Saltzer, p/c Gettysburg College

Loyalty (fs) by Bertram Saltzer, p/c Gettysburg College

GROVE CITY COLLEGE, Grove City

Alma Mater (am) by Pohlmann, arr. Cole, p/c Grove City College

Fight Song (fs) (Tune, Our Director March, refer to Song Sources)

HAVERFORD COLLEGE, Haverford

Alma Mater, Strong and True (am), no w/m credit given, p/c not listed

Ring Out the Good Old Song (fs) by Elliot Field, p/c Haverford College Book Store

Haverford Harmony Song (o) by Sigmund Spaeth, p/c Haverford College Book Store

Let's Go to Haverford (o) by Olga Wolf, arr. Sigmund Spaeth, p/c Haverford College Book Store

Vive La Haverford (o), no w/m credit given, arr. Wm. H. Reese, p/c Haverford College Book Store

When on the College Campus (o), no w/m credit given, arr. Weiler, arr. Wm. H. Reese, p/c Haverford College Book Store

Refer to *The Haverford College Song Book,* edited by William H. Reese, p/c Haverford College Book Store

IMMACULATA COLLEGE, Immaculata

Alma Mater (am) by Rev. Anthony J. Flynn (w) and Sister M. Immaculee, IHM, p/c not listed

INDIANA UNIVERSITY OF PENNSYLVANIA, Indiana

Alma Mater (am) by Hamlin E. Cogswell, arr. Charles A. Davis, p/c Indiana University of Pennsylvania

Fight Song (fs), no w/m credit given, arr. Charles A. Davis, p/c Indiana University of Pennsylvania

Cherokee (o) (Tune, Cherokee, refer to Song Sources)

Hail! Indiana (o) by Dr. Harold Orendorff, arr. Charles A. Davis, p/c Indiana University of Pennsylvania

JUNIATA COLLEGE, Huntingdon

To Juniata (am) by Frank B. Ward and C. L. Rowland, arr. Jim Martin and I. Brook Tower, p/c Hinds, Hayden & Eldredge, Inc. and [1926] Juniata College

Stand Up and Cheer (fs) (Tune, Stand Up and Cheer, refer to Song Sources), arr. E. Breitenfeld, p/c Hinds, Hayden & Eldredge, Inc.

Also refer to *Songs of Juniata* (Jubilee Edition), p/c Hinds, Hayden, & Eldredge, Inc. [1926]

KING'S COLLEGE, Wilkes-Barre

Hail to the Red and Gold (am) by Thomas Brogan, p/c King's College

We Are the Lions (fs) (Tune, Americans We, refer to Song Sources)

King's Fight Song (ofs) by Thomas Brogan, p/c King's College

KUTZTOWN UNIVERSITY OF PENNSYLVANIA, Kutztown

Alma Mater (am) (Tune, Aurelia, refer to Song Sources), Clyde Francis Lytle (wa), p/c not listed

Kutztown University Fight Song (fs) (Tune, When the Saints Go Marching In, refer to Song Sources)

Washington and Lee Swing (o) (refer to Song Sources)

LEBANON VALLEY COLLEGE, Annville

Alma Mater (am) by Max F. Lehman '07 (w) and Earle A. Spessard '11 (m), p/c copyright [1915] by Spessard and Lehman

LEHIGH UNIVERSITY, Bethlehem

Rearing, Tearing (fs) by E. S. Colling, p/c Lehigh University

LOCK HAVEN UNIVERSITY OF PENNSYLVANIA, Lock Haven

Alma Mater, Lock Haven University of Pennsylvania (am) by W. V. Routch, p/c Lock Haven University of Pennsylvania

Fight Song (fs) (Tune, The Victors, refer to Song Sources)

MANSFIELD UNIVERSITY OF PENNSYLVANIA, Mansfield

Mansfield, Hail (am) by Will George Butler, p/c Mansfield University of Pennsylvania

Red and Black (fs) no w/m credit given, p/c Mansfield University of Pennsylvania

Mansfield Victory (ofs) no w/m credit given, p/c Mansfield University of Pennsylvania

MILLERSVILLE UNIVERSITY OF PENNSYLVANIA, Millersville

Alma Mater (am) (Tune, Spanish Hymn, refer to Song Sources)

Fight Song (fs) (Tune, The Victors, refer to Song Sources)

MORAVIAN COLLEGE, Bethlehem

Moravian Alma Mater (am) (Tune, Annie Lisle, refer to Song Sources)

On, Moravian (fs) (Tune, On Wisconsin, refer to Song Sources)

MUHLENBERG COLLEGE, Allentown

Alma Mater (am) by E. H. Kister, arr. H. K. Marks, p/c Muhlenberg College

Fight Song (fs) (Tune, Put On Your Old Gray Bonnet, refer to Song Sources)

PENNSYLVANIA STATE UNIVERSITY, University Park

Penn State Alma Mater (am) by Fred Lewis Pattee, arr. Burden, p/c Pennsylvania State University

Fight On State (fs) by F. E. Wilbur (w) and Saunders (m), arr. Yoder, p/c Pennsylvania State University

The Nittany Lion (o) by Leyden, arr. Bilik, p/c Pennsylvania State University

Victory (o) by Leyden, arr. Bilik, p/c Pennsylvania State University

ROBERT MORRIS COLLEGE, Coraopolis

Hail to Thee, Dear Robert Morris (am), no w/m credit given, p/c not listed

SAINT FRANCIS COLLEGE, Loretto

Saint Francis College Alma Mater (am) by Ivan J. Washabaugh, p/c Saint Francis College

ST. VINCENT COLLEGE AND SEMINARY, Latrobe

St. Vincent (am) by Rev. Ignatius Groll, O.S.B., p/c St. Vincent College and Seminary

March of the Gold and Green (fs) by Rev. Thomas J. Quigley, p/c St. Vincent College and Seminary

SETON HILL COLLEGE, Greensburg

Seton Hill Alma Mater (am) (Tune, March of the Men of Harlech or Men of Harlech, refer to Song Sources), Daniel R. Sullivan (wa), p/c not listed. Present text revised in [1988] due to admission of male students to School of Fine Arts (music, theater, art, communication); second phrase changed to: "Sons and daughters come to meet thee" instead of "We thy daughters."

SHIPPENSBURG UNIVERSITY OF PENNSYLVANIA, Shippensburg

Alma Mater (am) (Tune, Annie Lisle, refer to Song Sources)

Hail to the Redskins (fs) (Tune, Hail to the Raiders), no w/m credit given, p/c not listed

SLIPPERY ROCK UNIVERSITY OF PENNSYLVANIA, Slippery Rock

Alma Mater (am), no w/m credit given, arr. D. Baker, p/c Slippery Rock University of Pennsylvania

Fight Song (fs) by B. Scarnati and A. Schmittlein (w) and J. Byers (m), p/c Slippery Rock University of Pennsylvania

SWARTHMORE COLLEGE, Swarthmore

Staunch and Gray (am) (Tune, Annie Lisle, refer to Song Sources), E. J. Taylor (wa), arr. H. L. Brown, p/c Swarthmore College

TEMPLE UNIVERSITY, Philadelphia

Alma Mater (am) by W. St. Clair (w) and C. D. Coppes (m), p/c Broadcast Music, Inc.

Fight! Temple Fight! (fs) by Maurice E. Swerdlow, p/c Broadcast Music, Inc.

UNIVERSITY OF PENNSYLVANIA, Philadelphia

Hail Pennsylvania (am) (Tune, Russian National Anthem, which anthem is not specified, refer to Song Sources)

Fight On, Pennsylvania (fs), no w/m credit given, arr. Lucien Caillet, p/c Elkan-Vogel

Cheer Pennsylvania (ofs) by C. W. O'Connor, p/c Hinds, Hayden & Eldredge, Inc.

Drink a Highball (o), no w/m credit given, p/c Broadcast Music, Inc.

Franklin Field (o) by Edwin Franko Goldman, p/c Elkan-Vogel

Hang Jeff Davis (o), no w/m credit given, arr. Lucien Caillet, p/c Elkan-Vogel

Men of Pennsylvania (o) by Clay Boland, p/c Edwin H. Morris & Co.

The Red and Blue (o), no w/m credit given, arr. Lucien Caillet, p/c Elkan-Vogel

U of P March (o) by Roland F. Seitz, p/c Roland F. Seitz

UNIVERSITY OF PITTSBURGH, Pittsburgh

Alma Mater (am) (Tune, by Franz Joseph Haydn, no title indicated), p/c not listed

Hail to Pitt (fs) by Harris, arr. Panella, p/c University of Pittsburgh Band

The Battle Song (o) by Harris, arr. Panella, p/c University of Pittsburgh Band

Bill Pitt Cheer for the Dear Old Lady (o) by Starrett, arr. Panella, p/c University of Pittsburgh Band

The Panther Song (o) by Harris, arr. Panella, p/c University of Pittsburgh Band

School Chant (o) by Harris and Rocereto, arr. Panella, p/c University of Pittsburgh Band

VILLANOVA UNIVERSITY, Villanova

Villanova University Anthem (am) by Al Dubin and Joe Burke, p/c J. W. Pepper and Son

V for Villanova (fs) by Les Irving, p/c Villanova University

March of the Wildcats (o) by McKeon, Gill, and Giordano, p/c J. W. Pepper and Son

Refer to *Songs of Villanova College,* arr. Paul Yoder, p/c J. W. Pepper and Son

WASHINGTON AND JEFFERSON COLLEGE, Washington

Washington and Jefferson (am) (Tune, Annie Lisle, refer to Song Sources)

Our Pledge (o) (Tune, Co-Ca-Che-Lunk, refer to Song Sources), F. P. Britt (wa), p/c not listed

WAYNESBURG COLLEGE, Waynesburg

Down Through the Ages (am), no w/m credit given, arr. Hall, p/c Waynesburg College

Fight Song (fs) (Tune, Washington and Lee Swing, refer to Song Sources)

WEST CHESTER UNIVERSITY OF PENNSYLVANIA, West Chester

West Chester Alma Mater (am) (Tune, Czarist National Anthem by Alexis Liadov, refer to Song Sources), arr. James R. Wells, p/c West Chester University of Pennsylvania

Ram's Fight (fs) by Paul Gerch, p/c West Chester University of Pennsylvania

WESTMINSTER COLLEGE, New Wilmington

Westminster Hymn (am) by G. B. Nevin, p/c Westminster College

Westminster Victory Song (fs) by Earl Johnson, arr. Herman W. Di Hoog, p/c Westminster College

WILKES UNIVERSITY, Wilkes-Barre

Alma Mater (am) by Eleanor Coates Farley, p/c Wilkes University

Wilkes Is in Town Again (fs) (Tune, In Town Again), no w/m credit given, p/c not listed

Wilkes Drinking Song (o) by Ted Warkomski, p/c Wilkes University

Wilkes Touchdown Song (o), no w/m credit given, p/c Wilkes University

YORK COLLEGE OF PENNSYLVANIA, York

Alma Mater (am), no w/m credit given, p/c not listed

RHODE ISLAND

BROWN UNIVERSITY, Providence

Alma Mater, We Hail Thee (am) (Tune, Araby's Daughter refer to Song Sources), arr. John Christie, p/c not listed

Ever True to Brown (fs) by Donald Jackson, p/c PD

Brown Cheering Song (o) by H. S. Young, p/c PD

Brown Forevermore (o) by Fred Otis, arr. Fred Otis and Martin Fischer, p/c PD

Chapel Steps (o) by G. C. Gow, arr. Martin Fischer, p/c PD

Commencement March (o) by D. W. Reeves, arr. John Christie, p/c PD

Ki-Yi-Yi (o) by Edward Corliss, p/c PD

BRYANT COLLEGE, Smithfield

Bryant College Alma Mater (am) (Tune, Annie Lisle, refer to Song Sources)

Bryant Senior Song (o) (Tune, Till We Meet Again, refer to Song Sources)

PROVIDENCE COLLEGE, Providence

Alma Mater (am) (Tune, Finlandia, refer to Song Sources)

RHODE ISLAND COLLEGE, Providence

Alma Mater (am) by Grace Bird and Helen Leavitt, p/c Rhode Island College

RHODE ISLAND COMMUNITY COLLEGE, Warwick

Our College Bands (am) by Walter Brownsword (w) and Arthur E. Chatfield (m), p/c Rhode Island Community College

SALVE REGINA, THE NEWPORT COLLEGE, Newport

Salve Regina (am) by S. M. Rosins, p/c Salve Regina, the Newport College

UNIVERSITY OF RHODE ISLAND, Kingston

University of Rhode Island Alma Mater (am), no w/m credit given, p/c not listed

Rhode Island Born (fs), no w/m credit given, p/c University of Rhode Island

Fight On, Rhode Island (ofs), no w/m credit given, p/c University of Rhode Island

SOUTH CAROLINA

BAPTIST COLLEGE, Charleston

Hail to Thee, O Baptist College (am) (Tune, English Folk Song, title not given), Dr. David Cuttino (wa), arr. Dr. David W. Cuttino, p/c not listed

Stand Up and Cheer (fs) by Steve Rich (m), arr. Steve Rich, p/c not listed

BENEDICT COLLEGE, Columbia

Benedict College Alma Mater (am) (Tune, O Tannenbaum, refer to Song Sources)

CLAFLIN COLLEGE, Orangeburg

Fight On Ole CU (am) (Tune, Annie Lisle, refer to Song Sources), Mrs. Aileen Southern (wa), p/c Claflin College

CLEMSON UNIVERSITY, Clemson

Clemson Alma Mater (am) by A. C. Corcoran (w) and Hugh McGarity (m), p/c Clemson University

Fight Song (fs) (Tune, Tiger Rag, refer to Song Sources)

COKER COLLEGE, Hartsville

Coker College, Hail to Thee (am) (Tune, Gaudeamus Igitur, refer to Song Sources), Class of 1960 (wa), p/c not listed

COLLEGE OF CHARLESTON, Charleston

Hail to Thee, Our Alma Mater (am), no w/m credit given, p/c not listed

CONVERSE COLLEGE, Spartanburg

Alma Mater (am), no w/m credit given, p/c Converse College

FURMAN UNIVERSITY, Greenville

Alma Mater (am) by Potcat, Barnes, and Ellis, p/c Furman University

Hail to White and Purple (fs) (Tune, Our Director March, refer to Song Sources)

LIMESTONE COLLEGE, Gaffney

Oh Limestone, Cherished Limestone (am) by F. L. Eyer, p/c F. L. Eyer

PRESBYTERIAN COLLEGE, Clinton

Alma Mater, Hail to Thee (am) by William P. Jacobs III, p/c Presbyterian College

On PC (fs) by Frances McSween, p/c Presbyterian College

SOUTH CAROLINA STATE COLLEGE, Orangeburg

Sing the Praises of Alma Mater (am) by R. S. Wilkinson (w) and Theodore D. Phillips (m), p/c South Carolina State College

Evening Song (o) by Reginald R. Thomasson, p/c South Carolina State College

UNIVERSITY OF SOUTH CAROLINA, Columbia

Here's a Health to Carolina (am), no w/m credit given, p/c University of South Carolina

USC Alma Mater (oam), by G. A. Wauchope, arr. Goodwin, p/c University of South Carolina

Carolina Fight Song (fs) (Tune, Step to the Rear, refer to Song Sources), Paul Dietzel (wa), arr. Rudolph, p/c not listed

When Irish Eyes Are Smiling (o) (refer to Song Sources)

WINTHROP COLLEGE, Rock Hill

Alma Mater (am) by Donna Durst and Lisa Breland (w) and Donna Durst (m), p/c Donna Durst

WOFFORD COLLEGE, Spartanburg

Alma Mater (am) (Tune, Annie Lisle, refer to Song Sources)

Fight Song (fs) (Tune, Michigan State Fight Song, refer to Song Sources)

SOUTH DAKOTA

AUGUSTANA COLLEGE, Sioux Falls

Augustana Alma Mater (am), no w/m credit given, arr. James Berdahl, p/c Augustana College

Augustana Rouser (fs) by Richard Svanoe, arr. Gerald Kemner, p/c Augustana College

Norwegian National Anthem (o) (Tune, Ja, Vi Elsker Dette Landet, refer to Song Sources)

DAKOTA STATE COLLEGE, Madison

DSC Alma Mater (am) by Berendsen, p/c Dakota State College

Fight Song (fs) (Tune, On Wisconsin, refer to Song Sources)

DAKOTA WESLEYAN UNIVERSITY, Mitchell

Scotchman (am) no w/m credit given, p/c Dakota Wesleyan University

Fight Song (fs) (Tune, Illinois Loyalty, refer to Song Sources)

HURON UNIVERSITY, Huron

Huron University Alma Mater (am) by Paul Royer, p/c Huron University

Huron Loyalty (fs), no w/m credit given, p/c Huron University

NORTHERN STATE UNIVERSITY, Aberdeen

Fight On for Northern (fs), no w/m credit given, arr. Philip L. Weinacht, p/c Northern State University

NSU Victory March (ofs), no w/m credit given, arr. Philip L. Weinacht, p/c Northern State University

Up Northern Wolves (ofs), no w/m credit given, arr. Philip L. Weinacht, p/c Northern State University

PRESENTATION COLLEGE, Aberdeen

Presentation College Alma Mater (am) (Tune, Pomp and Circumstance, refer to Song Sources)

SIOUX FALLS COLLEGE, Sioux Falls

Alma Mater (am) (Tune, Neapolitan Nights, refer to Song Sources)

Fight Song (fs) (Tune, Washington and Lee Swing, refer to Song Sources)

SOUTH DAKOTA SCHOOL OF MINES AND TECHNOLOGY, Rapid City

Fight Song (fs) (Tune, Ramblin' Wreck from Georgia Tech, refer to Song Sources)

SOUTH DAKOTA STATE UNIVERSITY, Brookings

Yellow and Blue (am) by Francis J. Haynes (w) and N. E. Hansen (m), p/c South Dakota State University

Ring the Bells (fs) by Stan Schleuter (w), no (m) credit given, p/c not listed

SOUTHERN STATE, Springfield

Fight Song (fs) (Tune, University of Minnesota Rouser, refer to Song Sources)

UNIVERSITY OF SOUTH DAKOTA, Vermillion

Alma Mater (am), no w/m credit given, p/c not listed

Hail South Dakota (fs) by W. F. Colton, p/c University of South Dakota

South Dakota Victory (ofs) no w/m credit given, p/c University of South Dakota

TENNESSEE

AUSTIN PEAY STATE UNIVERSITY, Clarksville

All Hail to Austin Peay (am) by Aaron Schmidt, p/c Dr. Aaron Schmidt

Smash Bang (fs) by Charles L. Gary, arr. Aaron Schmidt, p/c Dr. Aaron Schmidt/Austin Peay State University

Go Governors Go (o) by Charles L. Gary, arr. Aaron Schmidt, p/c Aaron Schmidt

BELMONT COLLEGE, Nashville

Belmont College Alma Mater (am) by F. Janet Wilson and Robert Mulloy (w/m), p/c Belmont College

Belmont Fight Song (fs) by Don Jackson, arr. Don Jackson, p/c Belmont College

CARSON-NEWMAN COLLEGE, Jefferson City

Alma Mater (am) (Tune, Annie Lisle, refer to Song Sources), John Campbell (wa), p/c not listed

Carson-Newman Fight Song (fs), no w/m credit given, arr. Joe Ray, p/c not listed

DAVID LIPSCOMB UNIVERSITY, Nashville

David Lipscomb Hail to Thee (am) by Pat Boone and Don Henley, p/c David Lipscomb University

Fight Song (fs) (Tune, Dixie, refer to Song Sources)

FREE WILL BAPTIST BIBLE COLLEGE, Nashville

Within These Halls (am) by Roos (w) and Clark (m), p/c National Association of Free Will Baptists (c) [1955]

LANE COLLEGE, Jackson

Fairlane (am) by Athal Smith, p/c Lane College

MEMPHIS STATE UNIVERSITY, Memphis

MSU Alma Mater (am), no w/m credit given, p/c not listed

Go, Tigers Go (fs) by Thos. Ferguson, p/c Memphis State University

MIDDLE TENNESSEE STATE UNIVERSITY, Murfreesboro

Alma Mater (am) by Douglas Williams, p/c Middle Tennessee State University

Blue Raiders Ride (fs) by Paul Yoder, p/c Middle Tennessee State University

MILLIGAN COLLEGE, Milligan College

Fair Milligan (am) (Tune, Annie Lisle, refer to Song Sources)

SOUTHERN COLLEGE OF SEVENTH-DAY ADVENTISTS, Collegedale

Collegedale Forever (am) by Margarita Dietel (w) and Marjorie Wynn-Hall (m), p/c not listed

Come On Down to Collegedale (recruitment song) (o) by John Thurber (w) and Wayne Thurber (m), p/c not listed

SOUTHWESTERN AT MEMPHIS, Memphis

Alma Mater (am) by Isaac Mason, arr. Burnet Tuthill, p/c Southwestern at Memphis

On the Prowl (fs) by R. L. Frank, p/c Southwestern at Memphis

Hail, Southwestern, Hail (o), no w/m credit given, arr. W. K. Dolen, p/c Southwestern at Memphis

Lynx March (o) by John Phillip Cooper, p/c Southwestern at Memphis

Onward, Southwestern (o), no w/m credit given, arr. W. K. Dolen, p/c Southwestern at Memphis

TENNESSEE STATE UNIVERSITY, Nashville

Alma Mater (am) by Laura M. Averitte (w) and Clarence H. Wilson (m), arr. Clarence H. Wilson, p/c not listed

TENNESSEE TECHNOLOGICAL UNIVERSITY, Cookeville

Tennessee Tech Hymn (am) by John Derryberry, arr. Wayne Pegram, p/c Tennessee Technological University

Tennessee Tech Fight Song (fs) by Paul Yoder, p/c Neil Kjos

TENNESSEE TEMPLE UNIVERSITY, Chattanooga

Through the Halls of Temple University (am), no w/m credit given, p/c Tennessee Temple University

TENNESSEE WESLEYAN COLLEGE, Athens

TWC Alma Mater (am) (Tune, Annie Lisle, refer to Song Sources)

UNION UNIVERSITY, Jackson

Alma Mater (am) by Kimsey-Hughes, arr. Hughes, p/c Union University

The Union Growler (fs) by C. Huffman, p/c Union University

UNIVERSITY OF TENNESSEE, Chattanooga

UTC Fight Song (fs) by Charles Carter, p/c University of Tennessee at Chattanooga

UNIVERSITY OF TENNESSEE, Knoxville

Alma Mater (am) by Meek, arr. Barry McDonald, p/c University of Tennessee Music Club

Rocky Top Tennessee (fs) by Bryant, p/c House of Bryant

Fight, Vols Fight (ofs) by Thornton W. Allen, arr. Barry McDonald, p/c Thornton W. Allen

Down the Field (ofs) (Tune, Down the Field, refer to Song Sources), arr. Barry McDonald

Spirit of the Hall (ofs) by Gooble-Meek, arr. Barry McDonald, p/c Carl Fischer, Inc.

VANDERBILT UNIVERSITY, Nashville

Alma Mater (am) (Tune, Annie Lisle, refer to Song Sources)

The Dynamite Song (also, When Vandy Starts to Fight!) (fs) by Francis Craig, p/c Edwin H. Morris & Co.

TEXAS

ABILENE CHRISTIAN UNIVERSITY, Abilene

Oh Dear Christian University (am) by Dr. G. C. Morlan (wa), arr. Leonard Burford, p/c Abilene Christian University

Let's Win This Game (fs) by Fitzgerald, p/c Abilene Christian University

AUSTIN COLLEGE, Sherman

The Crimson and Gold (am) by Clarence E. Dodge, p/c Austin College

Fight Song (fs) (Tune, On Wisconsin, refer to Song Sources)

BAYLOR UNIVERSITY, Waco

That Good Old Baylor Line (am), no w/m credit given, arr. Charles Brown, p/c Charles Brown (used by the Baylor Band)

That Good Old Baylor Line (oam), no w/m credit given, arr. Donald Moore, p/c Southern Music Co.

Saint's Fight (fs) (Tune, When the Saints Go Marching In, refer to Song Sources), p/c arr. Charles Brown

Baylor Fight Song (o), no w/m credit given, arr. Donald Moore, p/c Southern Music Co.

EAST TEXAS BAPTIST UNIVERSITY, Marshall

Loyal and True (am), no w/m credit given, arr. Charles Sharp, p/c East Texas Baptist University

Fight Song (fs) (Tune, When the Saints Go Marching In, refer to Song Sources)

EAST TEXAS STATE UNIVERSITY, Commerce

Alma Mater (am) (Tune, Annie Lisle, refer to Song Sources)

Corinne (fs) by Dr. Ray Luke, p/c East Texas State University

E. T. Fight Song (ofs), no w/m credit given, p/c not listed

HARDIN-SIMMONS UNIVERSITY, Abilene

Hardin-Simmons Anthem (am) by Stiles Anderson, p/c Thornton Allen (Associated Music Publishers, Inc.)

Parade of the Purple and Gold (fs) by Marion B. McClure, p/c Thornton Allen (Associated Music Publishers, Inc.)

HOWARD PAYNE UNIVERSITY, Brownwood

Alma Mater (am) (Tune, Annie Lisle, refer to Song Sources)

Jackets (fs), no w/m credit given, p/c Howard Payne University

LAMAR UNIVERSITY, Beaumont

Lamar Loyalty (am) by Rhodes Smart, p/c Lamar Tech

Big Red (fs) by Dr. C. A. Pete Wiley, p/c C. A. Wiley

MCMURRY UNIVERSITY, Abilene

Hail to McMurry (am) by T. Fry, p/c McMurry University

On McMurry (fs) (Tune, On Wisconsin, refer to Song Sources)

MIDWESTERN STATE UNIVERSITY, Wichita Falls

MSU Alma Mater (am) by Harold Walters, arr. N. D. Crews, p/c Midwestern State University

MSU Fight Song (fs) by Marion B. McClute, arr. N. D. Crews, p/c Midwestern University

NORTH TEXAS STATE UNIVERSITY, Denton

Glory to the Green (am) by Julia Smith, p/c North Texas State University

NT Fight Song (fs) no w/m credit given, p/c North Texas State University

ODESSA COLLEGE, Odessa

Odessa College Alma Mater (am) by Paul Peck, arr. Peter A. Figert, p/c Odessa College

Stand Up and Cheer (fs) by Peter A. Figert, p/c Odessa College

OUR LADY OF THE LAKE COLLEGE, San Antonio

O.L.L. Cheer Song (o) by M. A. Rodesney, p/c Our Lady of the Lake College

PAN AMERICAN UNIVERSITY, Edinburg

Alma Mater (am), no w/m credit given, p/c Pan American University

Fight You Broncos (fs) by Charles Magurean and Milo Sweet, p/c Pan American University

PRAIRIE VIEW A & M UNIVERSITY, Prairie View

Dear Prairie View (am) (Tune, Finlandia, refer to Song Sources), O. Anderson Fuller (wa), p/c not listed

Prairie View Fight Song (fs) by J. P. Mosley II, p/c Prairie View A & M University

Mighty Panther (ofs), no w/m credit given, p/c not listed

RICE UNIVERSITY, Houston

Rice's Honor (am) (Tune, Our Director March, refer to Song Sources)

The Rice Fight Song (fs) by Dr. Louis Girard, p/c Wm. Marsh Rice University

ST. EDWARD'S UNIVERSITY, Austin

Forever, SEU (am) by Bro. E. Reggio, arr. Bro. Daniel Kane, p/c St. Edward's University

SEU Fight (fs) by Bro. E. Reggio, p/c St. Edward's University

SAM HOUSTON STATE UNIVERSITY, Huntsville

Hail, Alma Mater (am) by Paul Yoder, p/c Edwin H. Morris & Co.

Fight Song (fs) (Tune, Semper Paratus, refer to Song Sources)

SAN JACINTO STATE COLLEGE, Pasadena

Hail to San Jacinto (am) by Dr. James B. Furrh, arr. Fred Baetge, p/c San Jacinto State College

San Jacinto Fight Song (fs) by Fred Baetge, p/c San Jacinto State College

SOUTHERN METHODIST UNIVERSITY, Dallas

Varsity (am), no w/m credit given, p/c Southern Methodist University

Peruna (fs) (Tune, Coming Around the Mountain, refer to Song Sources), arr. James Dreibrodt, p/c Oz Music Publishers

Go Mustangs, Go! (ofs) by Milo Sweet, p/c Edwin H. Morris & Co.

Pony Battle Cry (o) by James Dreibrodt, p/c Oz Music Publishers

SMU Loyalty Song (o) James Dreibrodt, p/c Oz Music Publishers

SOUTHWEST TEXAS STATE UNIVERSITY, San Marcos

SWT Alma Mater (am), no w/m credit given, arr. Doug Williamson, p/c Southwest Texas State University

Go! Bobcats (fs) by Paul Yoder, p/c Southwest Texas State University

Fight, You Bobcats (ofs) by Walter Willis, p/c Southwest Texas State University

SOUTHWESTERN UNIVERSITY, Georgetown

Hail, Alma Mater (am) by Edward Onstott, p/c not listed

STEPHEN F. AUSTIN STATE UNIVERSITY, Nacogdoches

Make Way for S.F.A. (am) by Fred Waring, p/c Stephen F. Austin State University

Leap Frog (fs) (refer to Song Sources)

TARLETON STATE UNIVERSITY, Stephenville

Tarleton Color Song (am), no w/m credit given, p/c not listed

On, Ye Tarleton (fs) (Tune, On Wisconsin, refer to Song Sources), H. A. Schmidt (w), p/c not listed

TEXAS A & I UNIVERSITY, Kingsville

Hail A & I (am), no w/m credit given, p/c Texas A & I University

Jalisco (fs), no w/m credit given, arr. J. L. Bellamah, p/c J. L. Bellamah

Fight, Fight for Ole A & I (ofs), no w/m credit given, p/c not listed

Javelina Victory March (o) by Noble Caine, p/c Belwin/Mills Publishing Corp.

TEXAS A & M UNIVERSITY, College Station

Spirit of Aggieland (am) by Marvin H. Mimms (w) and Colonel Richard J. Dunn (m), arrangement for band not published and is played exclusively by the Texas Aggie Band, p/c not listed

Texas Aggie War Hymn (fs) by J. V. Pinky Wilson, arr. Colonel Richard J. Dunn, p/c (former Students Association), (c) [1974]

TEXAS CHRISTIAN UNIVERSITY, Fort Worth

TCU Alma Mater Hymn (am) by Glenn Canfield, arr. Curtis Wilson, p/c Texas Christian University

TCU March (fs) by Claude Sammis, arr. Ralph Guenther, p/c Southern Music Co.

TEXAS SOUTHERN UNIVERSITY, Houston

Alma Mater (am) by C. A. Tolbert, p/c not listed

TSU Fight Song (fs), no w/m credit given, p/c not listed

Horned Frogs, We Are All for You (ofs) by Mrs. Butler Smiser (w) and Claude Sammis (m), p/c not listed

TEXAS TECH UNIVERSITY, Lubbock

The Matador Song (am) by Vic Williams, p/c Texas Tech University

Fight Raiders, Fight (fs) by Vic Williams and John Tatgenhorst, p/c Texas Tech University

TEXAS WOMAN'S UNIVERSITY, Denton

Alma Mater (am) (Tune, Russian National Anthem [1922], refer to Song Sources), by Mamie Walker (wa), p/c not listed

Fight Song (fs) (refer to Texas A & M)

UNIVERSITY OF HOUSTON (Downtown), Houston

Alma Mater (am) by Harmony Class of '42, p/c not listed

UNIVERSITY OF HOUSTON (University Park), Houston

Alma Mater (am) by Harmony Class of '42, p/c not listed.

Campus Chimes and Alma Mater (oam), no w/m credit given, arr. William Moffit, p/c Hal Leonard Music, Inc.

Fight Song (fs) by Forest Fountain (w) and Marion Ford (m), p/c not listed

Fight Song (ofs), no w/m credit given, arr. William Moffit, p/c Hal Leonard Music, Inc.

UNIVERSITY OF MARY HARDIN-BAYLOR, Belton

Baylor Hymn (am) by Dr. S. H. Luther, p/c Mary Hardin-Baylor University

Old Baylor Is Marching (fs) by Dorothy Moore, arr. Jim Miller, p/c Dorothy Moore

Centennial Song (o) by Dr. Bess Heironymus, arr. Yvonne Northrup, p/c Mary Hardin-Baylor University

Mary Hardin-Baylor University (o) by Margret Gooding, p/c Mary Hardin-Baylor University

Swing Song (o) by Bessie Bolbo, p/c Mary Hardin-Baylor University

Up with the Purple (A Senior and Alumni Song) (o), no w/m credit given, p/c Mary Hardin-Baylor University

UNIVERSITY OF NORTH TEXAS, Denison

Glory to the Green and White (am) by Charles Langford (w) and Julia Smith (m), p/c not listed

Fight, North Texas (fs) by Francis Stroup, p/c not listed

UNIVERSITY OF TEXAS, Arlington

UT Arlington Alma Mater (am) by Lucien Cailliet, p/c University of Texas at Arlington

Go Mavericks Go (fs) by Rich Powers, p/c University of Texas at Arlington

UNIVERSITY OF TEXAS, Austin

The Eyes of Texas (fs) and (am) (Tune, I've Been Working on the Railroad, refer to Song Sources)

Texas Fight Song (ofs) by Manning and Di Nino, p/c Southern Music Co., also published by Neil A. Kjos Music Co.

UNIVERSITY OF TEXAS, El Paso

The Eyes of Texas (am) (Tune, I've Been Workin' on the Railroad, refer to Song Sources), p/c Manning and Di Nino version published by Neil A. Kjos Music Co., also published by Southern Music Co.

Miners Fight (fs) (also, Texas Fight Song) by Manning and Di Nino, p/c Southern Music Co.

Texas Fight Song (ofs) by Manning and Di Nino, p/c Southern Music Co., also published by Neil A. Kjos Music Co.

UNIVERSITY OF TEXAS, San Antonio

Hail UTSA (am) by Alan Craven (w) and Joe Stuessy (m), arr. Joe Stuessy, p/c not listed (c) [1981]

Go Roadrunners, Go! (fs) by Joe Stuessy (w/m) and arr. Joe Stuessy, p/c not listed (c) [1981]

WEST TEXAS STATE UNIVERSITY, Canyon

Alma Mater (am) (Tune, Annie Lisle, refer to Song Sources)

On, On Buffaloes (fs) (Tune, On, On U of K [University of Kentucky], refer to Song Sources)

Bear Down You Buffaloes (o) by Given and Sweet, p/c Sweet Music Co.

Charge, Buffaloes (o) by Dick Winslow, p/c Sweet Music Co.

Go, Go, Go (o) by Dick Winslow, p/c Sweet Music co.

UTAH

BRIGHAM YOUNG UNIVERSITY, Provo

College Song (am) by Merrill McDonald, p/c not listed

The Cougar Song (fs) by Clyde D. Sandgren, p/c C. D. Sandgren

Alma Mater (ofs) by Glenn S. Potter (w) and Walt Daniels (m), p/c not listed

Fight You Cougars (o) by Ralph G. Laycock, p/c Brigham Young University

UNIVERSITY OF UTAH, Salt Lake City

Utah Man (am), no w/m credit given, p/c not listed

Fight Song (fs) (Tune, Solomon Levi, refer to Song Sources)

UTAH STATE UNIVERSITY, Logan

Across the Quad at Eventide (am) by Theo. M. Burton, p/c Utah State University

Scotsman (fs), no w/m credit given, p/c Utah State University

Are You from Dixie? (o) (refer to Song Sources)

USU Fight (o) by Knighton, arr. Max Dalby, p/c Utah State University

USU Triumphal (o) by Max Dalby, p/c Utah State University

WEBER STATE COLLEGE, Ogden

Purple and White (am) by Wm. Manning, arr. Johnson, p/c Weber State College

Weber State Fight (fs) by Don Threlkeld, p/c Weber State College

We Are the Wildcats (ofs), no w/m credit given, p/c not listed

Wildcat Walk (o) by Don Threlkeld, p/c Weber State College

VERMONT

CASTLETON STATE COLLEGE, Castleton

Castleton Anthem (am) by Robert Aborn, arr. Richard Diehl, p/c Castleton State College

UNIVERSITY OF VERMONT, Burlington

Champlain (am) by D. D. Fisher, M.D. (w) and C. S. Putnam (m), arr. H. R. Dane, p/c Theodore W. Allen Co. [1938] assigned to Broadcast Music, Inc. [1947]

Vermont Victorius (fs) by A. F. Furman, H. P. Sharples and L. F. Killick (w/m), p/c University of Vermont [1918], revision of lyrics submitted to the Alumni Office by Eric Mortensen '66, p/c University of Vermont

Universitas V. Montis (o) by David Cox (w) and Jane Oppenlander (m), p/c not listed

VERMONT TECHNICAL COLLEGE, Randolph Center

Vermont Technical College Alma Mater (am) by Leland Green, (wa) [1911], words revised by Russell Farnsworth [1970], (Tune, Orange and Black, refer to Song Sources)

VIRGINIA

BRIDGEWATER COLLEGE, Bridgewater

Bridgewater Fair (am) by E. T. Hildebrand, p/c Bridgewater College

Pep Song (fs) by Philip Trout, p/c Bridgewater College

COLLEGE OF WILLIAM AND MARY, Williamsburg

The William and Mary Alma Mater (am) (Tune, Annie Lisle, refer to Song Sources), Wilson (wa), arr. Varner, p/c College of William and Mary

The William and Mary Fight Song (fs), no w/m credit given, arr. Varner, p/c College of William and Mary

Tribe Fight Song (ofs), no w/m credit given, p/c not listed

The William and Mary Victory March (ofs) by Kennard, arr. Varner, p/c College of William and Mary

HAMPDEN-SYDNEY COLLEGE, Hampden-Sydney

The Hampden-Sydney Hymn (am), no w/m credit given p/c Hampden-Sydney College

Alma Mater (oam) by Sarah Collins Fernandis 1882 (am) and Chauncey Northern '24 (m), p/c not listed

Fight Song (fs), no w/m credit given, p/c Hampden-Sydney College

JAMES MADISON UNIVERSITY, Harrisonburg

Alma Mater (am) by Mary J. Slaughter, p/c Madison University

Alma Mater (oam) by James R. Riley, p/c not listed

NORFOLK STATE UNIVERSITY, Norfolk

Norfolk State University Alma Mater (am) by Dr. Carl W. Haywood, p/c not listed

Norfolk State University Fight Song (fs) by Paul Adams, p/c not listed

OLD DOMINION UNIVERSITY, Norfolk

Old Dominion Hail (am) by Robert Jager, p/c Robert Jager

Hail, Alma Mater (am) (same as above)

Blue and White Fight (fs) by Robert Jager, p/c Robert Jager

RADFORD UNIVERSITY, Radford

Radford University Alma Mater (am), no w/m credit given, p/c Radford University

Fight Song (fs) (Tune, Scotland the Brave, refer to Song Sources)

SHENANDOAH COLLEGE AND CONSERVATORY OF MUSIC, Winchester

Shenandoah (am) by Fred Dreher (w) and Stuart Moore [1941] (m), arr. C. R. McCandless, p/c not listed

UNIVERSITY OF RICHMOND, Richmond

Alma Mater (am) (Tune, Aura Lee, refer to Song Sources)

Spider Born (fs), no w/m credit given (Refer to the University of North Carolina), arr. J. Larkin, p/c not listed

Red and Blue (ofs), no w/m credit given, arr. J. Larkin, p/c University of Richmond

Spider Spirit (o) (Tune, Give Me That Old Time Religion, refer to Song Sources)

UNIVERSITY OF VIRGINIA, Charlottesville

The Good Old Song (am) (Tune, Auld Lang Syne, refer to Song Sources)

Rugby Road (fs) (Tune, Ramblin' Wreck from Georgia Tech, refer to Song Sources)

The Cavalier Song (ofs) by Fulton Lewis, Jr., arr. James Berdahl, p/c University of Virginia

VIRGINIA POLYTECHNIC INSTITUTE AND STATE UNIVERSITY, Blacksburg

Sing Praise to Alma Mater Dear (am), no w/m music credit given, p/c not listed

Tech Triumph (fs) by Goss and Maddux, arr. Yoder, p/c Virginia Polytechnic Institute and State University

VIRGINIA STATE UNIVERSITY, Petersburg

Virginia State University Alma Mater (am) by Austin Burleigh, p/c Virginia State University

Trojan's Victory March (fs) by Phil Medley, p/c Virginia State University

Forward to Victory (ofs) by Phil Medley, p/c Virginia State University

Evening Song (o) by Anderson, arr. Jackson, p/c verse only Virginia State University (Chorus, Carry Me Back to Old Virginny, refer to Song Sources)

WASHINGTON AND LEE UNIVERSITY, Lexington

Washington and Lee Swing (fs) (refer to Song Sources)

WASHINGTON

BIG BEND COMMUNITY COLLEGE, Moses Lake

Viking Victory March (fs) by Roy Hansen, p/c The Music Shop, Minneapolis, MN

CENTRAL WASHINGTON UNIVERSITY, Ellensburg

The Crimson and the Black (am), no w/m credit given, arr. Bert Christianson, p/c not listed

Fight for Ellensburg (fs) (Tune, Across the Field, from *The College Song Book,* refer to Song Sources), no w/m credit given, arr. Bert Christianson, p/c not listed

EASTERN WASHINGTON UNIVERSITY, Cheney

Alma Mater (am) by George W. Lotzenhiser (w), no (m) credit given, p/c not listed

GONZAGA UNIVERSITY, Spokane

Alma Mater (am), no w/m credit given, p/c not listed

Bulldogs of Gonzaga (fs) by John Burke (w) and James V. Monaco (m), arr. James V. Monaco, p/c Select Music Publications, Inc. [1937]

PACIFIC LUTHERAN UNIVERSITY, Tacoma

Alma Mater (am), no w/m credit given, p/c not listed

PLU Fight Song (fs), no w/m credit given, p/c not listed

SEATTLE PACIFIC UNIVERSITY, Seattle

SPU Alma Mater (am) (Tune, Annie Lisle, refer to Song Sources)

Follow the Falcons (fs) by Leon V. Metcalf, p/c Carl Fischer, Inc.

UNIVERSITY OF PUGET SOUND, Tacoma

Puget Sound Alma Mater (am), no w/m credit given, arr. Geoffrey Bergler, p/c not listed

Puget Sound Fight Song (fs), no w/m credit given, arr. Geoffrey Bergler, p/c not listed

UNIVERSITY OF WASHINGTON, Seattle

Alma Mater (am) by Riley Allen (w) and George Hager (m), p/c not listed

Bow Down to Washington (fs) by Lester J. Wilson, arr. Kechley, p/c Panella Music Co.

Vict'ry for Washington (ofs) by Tom Herbert (w) and George Larson (m), p/c not listed

Bells of Washington (o) by Edmond S. Meany (w) and Carl Paige Wood (m), p/c Edwin H. Morris & Co.

WALLA WALLA COLLEGE, College Place

Walla Walla College Song by Hayes Davis (w) and Melvin Rees (m), p/c not listed

WASHINGTON STATE UNIVERSITY, Pullman

Washington State Alma Mater (am) by Phyllis Sayles, p/c Hanson Publications

Washington, My Washington (oam) by J. De Forest Cline, p/c not listed

Washington State Fight Song (fs) by J. De Forest Cline, p/c Hanson Publications

All Hail to Washington State (ofs) by Carl Minor, p/c Washington State University

Cougar Conquest (ofs) by Paul Yoder, p/c Neil A. Kjos Music Co.

WESTERN WASHINGTON UNIVERSITY, Bellingham

White and Blue (am) (Tune, Annie Lisle, refer to Song Sources), Ada Hogle Abbott (wa), p/c not listed

The Viking Victory March (fs) (Tune, The Victors, refer to Song Sources), Don Walter (wa), p/c not listed

WHITMAN COLLEGE, Walla Walla

Whitman! Here's to You! (am) by S.B.L. Penrose (w/m), arr. E. Blum, p/c Whitman College [1918]

WEST VIRGINIA

APPALACHIAN BIBLE INSTITUTE, Bradley

The Prayer of A.B.I. (am) by Mrs. L. E. Pipkin, arr. L. Shepard, p/c Appalachian Bible Institute

BETHANY COLLEGE, Bethany

Alma Mater (am) Jack Colburn (w) and Blair Burkhart (m), p/c Bethany College

Fite, Fite, Old Bethany (fs), no w/m credit given, p/c Bethany College

The Banks of the Old Buffalo (o), no w/m credit given, p/c Bethany College Book Store

Refer to *The First Book of Bethany Songs,* p/c Lea and Reeves in [1893]. Revised in [1923] and published by the Bethany College Bookstore. The book is available on loan through the Bethany College Library.

CONCORD COLLEGE, Athens

Hail, Concord College (am), no w/m credit given, p/c not listed

Let's Win This Game (fs) by Bernard Fitzgerald, p/c Neil A. Kjos Music Co.

FAIRMONT STATE COLLEGE, Fairmont

Among the Hills of Time (am), no w/m credit given, p/c not listed

FSC Fight Song (fs), no w/m credit given, p/c not listed

MARSHALL UNIVERSITY, Huntington

Marshall Alma Mater (am), no w/m credit given, p/c not listed

Sons of Marshall (fs) by E. Williams, arr. Paul Jennings, p/c Marshall University

Fight On (ofs), no w/m credit given, p/c not listed

ROANOKE COLLEGE, Salem

Deep in Our Hearts (am) by Frank M. Williams, p/c Frank M. Williams

SALEM-TEIKYO UNIVERSITY, Salem

Alma Mater (am) (Tune, Annie Lisle, refer to Song Sources)

Fight Song (fs) (Tune, Tiger Rag, refer to Song Sources)

SHEPHERD COLLEGE, Shepherdstown

Alma Mater (am) (Tune, Annie Lisle, refer to Song Sources)

Fight on SC (fs) (Tune, Fight On, refer to Song Sources)

Onward Shepherd (o) (Tune, On Wisconsin, refer to Song Sources)

WEST LIBERTY STATE COLLEGE, West Liberty

Alma Mater (am) (Tune, Integer Vitae, refer to Song Sources)

WEST VIRGINIA INSTITUTE OF TECHNOLOGY, Montgomery

Fight-Em, Bite-Em (fs) by A. Nunley, arr. C. Martyn, p/c West Virginia Institute of Technology

WEST VIRGINIA STATE COLLEGE, Institute

Alma Mater of West Virginia State College (am) by Ernest Wade and Virginia Spencer, p/c not listed

Hail to the Team (fs) by Fannin S. Belcher (w) and Joseph W. Grider (m), p/c not listed

WEST VIRGINIA UNIVERSITY, Morgantown

Alma, Our Alma Mater (am) by Louis D. Corson, p/c West Virginia University

Hail, West Virginia (fs) by Earl Miller and Ed McWhorter, p/c West Virginia University

Fight, Mountaineers (o), no w/m credit given, arr. Budd Udell, p/c West Virginia University

WEST VIRGINIA WESLEYAN COLLEGE, Buckhannon

Alma Mater of the Mountains (am) (Tune from Lucia di Lammermoor)

Here's to Old Wesleyan (fs), no w/m credit given, p/c West Virginia Wesleyan College

WHEELING JESUIT COLLEGE, Wheeling

Above the Ohio (am) by E. Gannon, S.J., p/c Wheeling Jesuit College

WISCONSIN

ALVERNO COLLEGE, Milwaukee

Alverno (am) by Sister Theophane Hytrek, p/c Alverno College

Winds of Alverno (fs) by Sister Theophane Hytrek, p/c Alverno College

BELOIT COLLEGE, Beloit

Dominie Salvan FAC (am) by Gounod, p/c PD

Gold Victory Song (fs) by Huffer and Lhotak, p/c Beloit College

Alma Mater Alumnus (o) by Grown and Olds, p/c PD

Beloit! All Hail! (o) by W. B. Olds, p/c PD

The Chapel Bell (o) by Faville and Thomas, p/c PD

The Prof (o) by W. B. Olds, p/c PD

CARTHAGE COLLEGE, Kenosha

Alma Mater (am) by Engel, arr. Roth, p/c not listed

Carthage Fight Song (fs), no w/m credit given, arr. Karvonen, p/c not listed

LAKELAND COLLEGE, Sheboygan

Alma Mater (am) by F. W. Knatz, p/c not listed

Muskie Victory (fs) by Edgar Thiessen, p/c not listed

LAWRENCE UNIVERSITY, Appleton

Alma Mater (am) by Mrs. Rush Winslow (w) and Louis R. Dressler (m), p/c not listed

Viking Song (fs) by La Vahn Maesch and Fred Trezise, p/c not listed

MARQUETTE UNIVERSITY, Milwaukee

Marquette University Anthem (am) by Liborius Semmann, p/c not listed

Ring Out Ahoya! (fs) by Olive Glueckstein '29, p/c not listed

MOUNT MARY COLLEGE, Milwaukee

Sing to Our Fair Alma Mater (am) by Sister M. Francele, p/c Mount Mary College

NORTHWESTERN COLLEGE, Watertown

Hail to Thee (am), no w/m credit given, arr. Arnold O. Lehmann, p/c Northwestern College

Cheer for Old Northwestern (fs) by C. Bolle and R. Bolle, arr. Arnold O. Lehmann, p/c Northwestern College

ST. NORBERT COLLEGE, De Pere

Varsity Toast (am) by Norbert J. Ecker, p/c St. Norbert College

UNIVERSITY OF WISCONSIN, Eau Claire

University Hymn (am) (Tune, We Praise Thee, O God, refer to Song Sources)

Blue Gold Fight Song (fs) (Tune, NC-4 March, refer to Song Sources)

UNIVERSITY OF WISCONSIN, Green Bay

Alma Mater (am), no w/m credit given, p/c not listed

UNIVERSITY OF WISCONSIN, La Crosse

Alma Mater (am), no w/m credit given, p/c not listed

La Crosse (fs) by Joyce Grill, p/c Joyce Grill (c) [1987]

UNIVERSITY OF WISCONSIN, Madison

Varsity, Varsity (am), no w/m credit given, p/c not listed

On, Wisconsin (fs) by Carl Beck (w) and W. T. Purdy (m), p/c Edwin H. Morris & Co.

UNIVERSITY OF WISCONSIN, Milwaukee

UWM Alma Mater (am) by Ralph Hermann, p/c Ralph Hermann

UWM Fight Song (fs) by Ralph Hermann, p/c Ralph Hermann

UNIVERSITY OF WISCONSIN, Oshkosh

Hail Alma Mater (am) by J. A. Breese, p/c not listed

Hail Titans (fs) by J. A. Breese, p/c not listed

UNIVERSITY OF WISCONSIN, Parkside

Parkside Fight Song (fs) by Wegner-Thomason, p/c not listed

UNIVERSITY OF WISCONSIN, Platteville

Alma Mater Grand and Glorious (am), no w/m credit given, p/c not listed

Fight Song (fs), no w/m credit given, p/c not listed

UNIVERSITY OF WISCONSIN, River Falls

Pledge Song (am) by Marvin Geers, p/c University of Wisconsin, River Falls

Falcon Victory (fs) by John Radd, p/c University of Wisconsin, River Falls

Falls March (o) by William Eller, p/c William Eller [1908]

UNIVERSITY OF WISCONSIN, Stevens Point

The Purple and the Gold (am), no w/m credit given, p/c not listed

Fight Song (fs) (Tune, same as University of Kentucky)

UNIVERSITY OF WISCONSIN/STOUT, Menomonie

Alma Mater to the Stout Institute (am), no w/m credit given, p/c not listed

School Fight Song (fs), no w/m credit given, p/c not listed

UNIVERSITY OF WISCONSIN, Superior

To Thee We Sing (am) by Bernice Robinson and Virginia McKie (w/m), p/c not listed

Orange and Black (fs) by Jean Nelson, Barbara Rauchenstein, and Ruth Johnson (w/m), p/c not listed

UNIVERSITY OF WISCONSIN, Whitewater

Whitewater Alma Mater (am), no w/m credit given, p/c not listed

Warhawk Fight Song (fs) by Roberts, arr. Rohrs, p/c not listed

Warhawk Battle Cry (o) by Paul Yoder, p/c Loop Publishing Co.

VITERBO COLLEGE, La Crosse

Viterbo, Dear Old Alma Mater (am) by Joyce Grill, p/c Viterbo College [1990]

We're Viterbo (fs) by Joyce Grill, p/c Viterbo College [1990]

WISCONSIN STATE UNIVERSITY, La Crosse

Alma Mater (am) (Tune, Annie Lisle, refer to Song Sources), arr. Paul Yoder, p/c Neil A. Kjos Music Co.

Fight Song (fs) (Tune, On Wisconsin and The Beer Barrel Polka, refer to Song Sources)

WYOMING

EASTERN WYOMING COLLEGE, Torrington

E.W.C. Fight Song (fs) by Carrol Butts, p/c Eastern Wyoming College

NORTHWEST COMMUNITY COLLEGE, Powell

Fight Song (fs) (Tune, Hey, Look Me Over, refer to Song Sources)
Fight Song (ofs) (Tune, Hail Purdue, refer to Song Sources)

UNIVERSITY OF WYOMING, Laramie

Alma Mater (am), no w/m credit given, arr. F. J. Lewis, p/c not listed
Cowboy Joe (fs), no w/m credit given, p/c PD

Song Sources

ACADEMIC FESTIVAL OVERTURE by Johannes Brahms, p/c [1879]

ACROSS THE FIELD by W. A. Dougherty, Jr., p/c Edwin H. Morris & Co.

AGGIE FIGHT SONG (refer to OH DIDN'T HE RAMBLE)

AGGIE WAR HYMN by J. V. "Pinky" Wilson (w/m) (c) [1921], arr. R. Dunn, p/c Southern Music Co.

AMERICANS WE by Henry Fillmore, p/c Carl Fischer, Inc.

AMERICA THE BEAUTIFUL (Tune, MATERNA by Samuel Augustus Ward), Katherine Lee Bates (w). The words were first published in the weekly periodical *The Congregationalist,* Boston, July 4, 1895. The tune MATERNA is set to the words of O MOTHER DEAR, JERUSALEM, which appeared in *The Parish Choir,* Boston, July 12, 1888.

AMICI no w/m credit given (see ANNIE LISLE, identical except for slight variance at B section), traditional, p/c PD

ANCHORS AWEIGH by A. H. Miles and R. Lovell (w) and Charles A. Zimmerman (m), p/c Ida M. Zimmerman [1906], assigned to Robbins Music (Big 3 Music Corp.)

ANNIE LISLE by H. S. Thompson (tune used by Cornell University with the title FAR ABOVE CAYUGA'S WATERS), p/c Oliver Ditson and Co., Boston [1860]

ARABY'S DAUGHTER by Thomas Moore (w) and George Kiallmark (m), p/c James L. Hewitt & Co., Boston [ca. 1826]. The words are derived from "The Fire-Worshippers," the third of the four tales that comprise Moore's *Lalla Rookh,* published in London [1817]. The music was adapted to Samuel Woodworth's poem "The Old Oaken Bucket."

ARE YOU FROM DIXIE? by Jack Yellen (w) and George L. Cobb (m), p/c not listed [ca. 1915]

THE ARMY AIR CORPS (refer to the U.S. Air Force)

THE ARMY GOES ROLLING ALONG (Tune, THE CAISSONS GO ROLLING ALONG) (refer to The United States FIELD ARTILLERY MARCH)

AS THE BACKS GO TEARING BY (Dartmouth) by Thomas Keady (w) and Carl W. Blaisdell (m), p/c PD

ATLANTIC SQUADRON by R. B. Hall, p/c John Church

AULD LANG SYNE (Tune, a traditional Scottish tune with words adapted by Robert Burns; the present melody appears to be a composite of several Scottish tunes), p/c Preston & London [1799]

AUPRES DE MA BLONDE no w/m credit given, traditional French air, p/c (c) [1580] PD

AURA LEE by W. W. Fosdick (w) and George R. Poulton (m), p/c John Church, Jr. (c.) [1861]

AURELIA no w/m credit given, p/c PD

AUSTRIAN NATIONAL ANTHEM (refer to GOTT MIR DIR MEIN OSTER-REICH or OSTERREICHISCHE BUNDESHYMNE and *NATIONAL ANTHEMS OF THE WORLD,* edited by Martin Shaw and Henry Coleman), p/c Pitman Publishing Corp. [1960]. Most responses did not specify exact titles, and it is recommended that all national anthems be checked through the school in question because historical and political changes can present two or more options.

BARNUM AND BAILEY'S FAVORITE by Karl King, p/c C. L. Barnhouse & Co.

BATTLE HYMN OF THE REPUBLIC by Julia Ward Howe (w) [written in 1861] GLORY, (tune, GLORY, GLORY HALLELUJAH by William Steffe, published anon.), p/c Oliver Ditson & Co., Boston [1862]

BEAR DOWN ARIZONA by Jack Lee, p/c Hal Leonard Publishing Corp.

THE BEER BARREL POLKA by Lew Brown, Wladimir A. Timm, and Jaromir Vejvoda (w/m), p/c Shapiro, Bernstein & Co., Inc., (c) [1934] by Jana Hoffmanna, assigned and copyrighted [1939] by Shapiro, Bernstein & Co., Inc.

BELIEVE ME IF ALL THOSE ENDEARING YOUNG CHARMS by Thomas Moore (w) (Tune, My Lodging is on the Cold Ground, traditional Irish melody), p/c J. Power's Music & Instrument Warehouse, London [1808]

THE BELLS OF ST. MARY'S by Douglas Furber (w) and A. Emmett Adams (m), p/c Chappell & Co., Ltd., London, (c) by Ascherberg, Hopwood & Crew, Ltd., London [1917]

BETHANY SONGS (FIRST BOOK OF) p/c Lea and Reeves [1893], revised [1923] and published by the Bethany College Bookstore. The book is available on loan through the Bethany College Library, WV.

THE BIG RED TEAM by Charles Tourison, arr. J. S. Seredey, p/c Carl Fischer, Inc.

THE BILLBOARD MARCH by John N. Klohr (m), p/c John Church Co. [1901] (Theodore Presser Co.)

BLAZE AWAY by Abe Holzmann (m), p/c Feist & Frankenthaler [1901] (Big 3 Music Corp.)

BLUE SKIRT WALTZ by V. Blaha, p/c Belwin-Mills Publishing Corp.

BRIGHT COLLEGE YEARS (refer to OH, BRING HOME THE WAGON, JOHN)

BRING HOME THE WAGON, JOHN, (Refer to Oh Bring Home the Wagon, John)

BRITISH EIGHTH MARCH by Z. Elliott, arr. Luckhardt, p/c Carl Fischer Co.

THE BULL DOG (BULLDOG! BULLDOG! BOW, WOW, WOW) by Cole Porter, p/c not listed [1911]

THE CAISSONS GO ROLLING ALONG (also, THE ARMY GOES ROLLING ALONG) by Brig. Gen. E. L. Gruber, p/c PD

THE CANADIAN NATIONAL ANTHEM (refer to O, CANADA). Most responses did not specify exact title, and it is recommended that all national anthems be checked through the school in question because historical and political changes can present two or more options.

CANNIBALEE by B. A. Gould, Jr. (w) and M. A. Taylor (m), p/c PD

CARMINA PRINCETONIA: The Songbook of Princeton University, edited by a university committee, p/c G. Schirmer, Inc.

CARRY ME BACK TO OLD VIRGINNY by James A. Bland, p/c John Perry & Co. [1878]

CHEROKEE by Ray Noble, p/c Shapiro, Bernstein and Co., Inc.

CHESTER (Tune, LET TYRANTS SHAKE THEIR IRON ROD) by William Billings, p/c Draper and Folsom, Boston [1778]

CHRISTE SANCTORUM 10 11 11 6 (Antiphone, Paris) [1681]

CHRISTIAN HYMN from WARTBURG COLLEGE HYMN BOOK, p/c Wartburg College, Waverly, IA

CO-CA-CHE-LUNK no w/m credit given, traditional, p/c PD

COLLECTION/CARMINA PRINCETONIA (refer to CARMINA PRINCETONIA)

THE COLLEGE SONG BOOK p/c Central Washington University, Ellensburg, WA

COLLEGE SONGS OF N.C. edited by Hazelman, p/c Brodt Music Co.

COMING AROUND THE MOUNTAIN (Tune traditional black American melody, WHEN THE CHARIOT COMES [1899 or earlier]), p/c PD

CORCORAN CADETS MARCH by John Philip Sousa, p/c PD

THE CORONATION MARCH (from "Le Prophete") by G. Meyerbeer, p/c PD

CZARIST NATIONAL ANTHEM by Alexis Liadov (refer to NATIONAL ANTHEMS OF THE WORLD, edited by Martin Shaw and Henry Coleman, p/c Pitman Publishing Corp. [1960]). Most responses did not specify exact titles, and it is recommended that all national anthems be checked through the school in question because historical and political changes can present two or more options.

DANKGEBET (refer to PRAYER OF THANKSGIVING)

DANNY BOY, by Frederick Edward Weatherly (w) (tune, adapted from an old Irish air by Frederick Edward Weatherly), p/c Boosey & Co., London [1913], renewed by Mrs. Miriam Weatherly [1941], assigned to Boosey & Hawkes, Inc., London [1941]

DEUTSCHLAND UBER ALLES by Joseph Haydn (1732–1809) (refer to NATIONAL ANTHEMS OF THE WORLD, edited by Martin Shaw and Henry Coleman, p/c Pittman Publishing Corp. [1960]). Most responses did not specify exact titles, and it is recommended that all national anthems be checked through the school in question because historical and political changes can present two or more options.

DIE WACHT AM RHEIN (THE WATCH ON THE RHINE) by Carl Wilhelm, p/c PD

DIXIE (also known as DIXIE'S LAND and I WISH I WAS IN DIXIE'S LAND) by Daniel Decatur Emmett, arr. W. L. Hobbs, p/c Firth, Pond & Co. [1860], PD

DOMINIE SALVAM by Charles Gounod, p/c PD

DOWN MAIN STREET by Weidt, arr. Hildreth, p/c Big 3 Music Corp.

DOWN THE FIELD by C. W. O'Connor (w) and Stanleigh P. Freedman (m), p/c Leo Feist, Inc. [1911]

DOWN THE LINE by Vincent F. Fagan (w) and Joseph J. Casasanta (m), p/c Melrose Music Corp. [1926] (Edwin H. Morris & Co.)

DOWN THE STREET by Victor Grabel, p/c C. L. Barnhouse Co.

DRAGONS' GOLDEN JUBILEE by Arnold M. Christensen, p/c C. L. Barnhouse Co.

DUTCH NATIONAL ANTHEM (refer to NATIONAL ANTHEMS OF THE WORLD, edited by Martin Shaw and Henry Coleman, p/c Pitman Publishing Corp. [1960]). It is recommended that all national anthems be checked through the school in question because historical and political changes can present two or more options.

1812 OVERTURE by Pyotr I. Tchaikovsky, p/c PD

ETERNAL FATHER, STRONG TO SAVE by John Dykes [1823–1876] (w) (Tune, MELITA, traditional), p/c PD

FAITH OF OUR FATHERS by Frederick William Faber [1814–1863] (w) and Henry F. Hemy [1813–1888] (m), adapted by James G. Walton [1821–1905], p/c PD

FAR ABOVE CAYUGA'S WATERS (refer to ANNIE LISLE)

FIELD ARTILLERY MARCH (refer to UNITED STATES FIELD ARTILLERY MARCH)

FIGHT ON (for USC) by Milo Sweet and Glen Grant, p/c Edwin H. Morris & Co.

FIGHT WILD CATS, FIGHT by Doug Holsclaw, p/c Associated Music Publishers, Inc. (Thornton W. Allen)

FINLANDIA (symphonic poem) by Jan Sibelius (m), p/c Breitkopf & Hartel, Leipzig [1901]

FIRST BOOK OF BETHANY SONGS p/c Bethany College Bookstore, Bethany, WV

GAUDEAMUS IGITUR (Tune, 18th-century German melody popularized by [1782], words possibly from [1287] Latin ms. and might well be the oldest student melody), p/c PD

GIVE ME THAT OLD TIME RELIGION no w/m credit given, traditional, p/c PD

GLORIFICATION MARCH by George Rosenkrans, p/c PD

GLORY, GLORY HALLELUJAH (refer to BATTLE HYMN OF THE REPUBLIC)

GLORY HAST THOU (refer to DEUTSCHLAND UBER ALLES)

GOD OF OUR FATHERS by Daniel C. Roberts [1841–1907] (w) and George W. Warren [1828–1902] (m), p/c PD

GO RAIDERS, GO by Henry Fillmore, p/c Carl Fischer, Inc.

GOTT MIR DIR MEIN OESTERREICH (refer to OSTERREICHISCHE BUNDESHYMNE) found in the INTERNATIONAL SONG BOOK, p. 17, p/c M. M. Cole Publishing Co. Most responses did not specify exact titles, and it is recommended that all national anthems be checked through the school in question because historical and political changes can present two or more options.

GO U NORTHWESTERN by Theo. C. Van Etten, arr. Harry Alford, p/c Edwin H. Morris & Co.

HAIL PURDUE by J. Morrison and E. J. Wotawa, arr. Harry Alford, p/c Edwin H. Morris & Co.

HAIL TO THE SPIRIT OF MIAMI U by Clark and Kennedy, arr. Henry Fillmore, p/c University of Miami

HAIL TO THE VARSITY by Paul Yoder, p/c Rubank, Inc.

HARVARD MARCH by Alfred G. Chaffee, p/c PD

HAVERFORD COLLEGE SONG BOOK edited by William Reese, p/c Haverford College Book Store, Haverford, PA

HAWAIIAN WAR CHANT by Ralph Freed (w) and Johnny Noble and Leleiohaku (m), p/c Sherman, Clay & Co. [1936], Miller Music Corp. [1938]

HAWAII FIVE-O by Stevens, p/c Hal Leonard Publishing Corp.

HERE'S TO OUR DEAR HAWAII by J. S. Zamecnik, p/c Sam Fox Publishing Co.

HEY, LOOK ME OVER by Carolyn Leigh (w) and Cy Coleman (m), p/c Moreley Music Co., Inc., (c) [1960] by Carolyn Leigh and Cy Coleman, selling agent Edwin H. Morris & Co., Inc.

HOW CAN I LEAVE THEE? (Tune, ACHE WIE IST'S MOGLICH) by Friedrich Kucken, p/c F. D. Benteen, Baltimore [1851]

ILLINOIS LOYALTY by Guild, p/c Edwin H. Morris & Co.

I'M A JAYHAWK by Bowles, arr. Gori, p/c Edwin H. Morris & Co.

INDIANA, OUR INDIANA by Russell P. Harker and Karl L. King, p/c Edwin H. Morris & Co.

INTEGER VITAE (from XXII ODE by Horace) (sometimes sung to PRAISE FOR PEACE), Angus S. Hibbard (translation and adaptation) and Friedrich F. Flemming [1778–1813] (m), p/c PD

INTERNATIONAL SONG BOOK p/c M. M. Cole Publishing Co.

IT'S A LONG, LONG WAY TO TIPPERARY by Jack Judge (w) and Harry M. Williams (m), p/c Chappell & Co., Ltd., London, (c) B. Feldman & Co., London [1912]

IT'S GREAT TO BE A TROJAN by Broadwell, p/c Oz Music Publishers

I'VE BEEN WORKING ON THE RAILROAD no w/m credit given, traditional, p/c PD

JA, VI ELSKER DETTE LANDET [Norwegian National Anthem], (refer to NATIONAL ANTHEMS OF THE WORLD, edited by Martin Shaw and Henry Coleman, p/c Pitman Publishing Corp. [1960]). Most responses did not specify exact titles, and it is recommended that all national anthems be checked through the school in question because historical and political changes can present two or more options.

JOLI BLONDE (refer to AUPRES DE MA BLONDE)

JOYCE'S 71st N.Y. REGIMENT by Boyer, p/c Carl Fischer, Inc.

LANCASHIRE by H. F. Moore (w) and Henry Smart, p/c not listed, PD

LAND OF HOPE AND GLORY (refer to POMP AND CIRCUMSTANCE)

LEAP FROG by Joe Garland, p/c MCA

LIGHTS OUT MARCH by McCoy, p/c Carl Fischer, Inc.

LONDONDERRY AIR (also, DANNY BOY), by Frederick Edward Weatherly (w), (tune, adapted from an old Irish air) by Frederick Edward Weatherly, p/c Boosey & Co., London (c) [1913], renewed by Mrs. Miriam Weatherly [1941], assigned to Boosey & Hawkes, Inc., London [1941]

LORENA by Rev. H.D.L. Webster (w) and Joseph Philbrick Webster (m), p/c Higgins Bros., Chicago [1857]

MARCHE SLAV by Pyotr I. Tchaikovsky, p/c PD

MARCH OF THE MEN OF HARLECH, Welsh poem translated by William Dutbie in original version (Tune, a Welsh air), p/c PD

MARINE'S HYMN no w/m credit given, p/c PD

MARYLAND! MY MARYLAND! (Tune, O TANNENBAUM!) by James Ryder Randall (w), p/c Miller & Beacham [1861]

MEN OF HARLECH (refer to MARCH OF THE MEN OF HARLECH)

MEN OF OHIO by Henry Fillmore, p/c Fillmore Music House (Carl Fischer, Inc),

THE MERMAID no w/m credit given, traditional (Tune, LEVERING, sea chantey), p/c PD

MICHIGAN STATE FIGHT SONG by Lankey, arr. Leonard Falcone, p/c Associated Music Publishers, Inc. (Thornton W. Allen)

MINNESOTA ROUSER by Floyd M. Hutsell, arr. Frank Bencriscutto, p/c Edwin H. Morris & Co.

MY BONNIE LASSIE (refer to SCOTLAND THE BRAVE)

NATIONAL ANTHEMS OF THE WORLD, edited by Martin Shaw and Henry Coleman, p/c Pitman Publishing Corp. [1960]

THE NAVY BLUE AND WHITE (refer to SADIE RAY)

THE NAVY HYMN (refer to ETERNAL FATHER, STRONG TO SAVE)

NC-4 MARCH by Bigelow, p/c Big 3 Music Corp.

NEAPOLITAN NIGHTS by Harry D. Kerr (w) and J. S. Zamecnik (m), p/c Sam Fox Publishing Co.

NEW COLONIAL MARCH by R. B. Hall, p/c John Church Co. (Theodore Presser & Co.)

NEW YORK UNIVERSITY SONG BOOKS p/c New York University, 70 Washington Square South, New York, NY 10012

NORWEGIAN NATIONAL ANTHEM, "Ja, vi elsker dette landet," (refer to NATIONAL ANTHEMS OF THE WORLD, edited by Martin Shaw and Henry Coleman, p/c Pitman Publishing Corp. [1960]). Most responses did not specify exact titles, and it is recommended that all national anthems be checked through the school in question because historical and political changes can present two or more options.

THE NOTRE DAME VICTORY MARCH by John Shea (w) and Michael Shea (m), p/c Edwin H. Morris & Co.

O, CANADA (CANADIAN NATIONAL ANTHEM) by C. Lavallee, p/c George V. Thompson, Ltd., Toronto, Canada. Most responses did not specify exact titles, and it is recommended that all national anthems be checked through the school in question because historical and political changes can present two or more options.

O GOD OF GRACE by Joseph Haydn, p/c PD

ODE TO JOY (Tune, NINTH SYMPHONY by Ludwig van Beethoven), p/c PD

ODE TO OLD UNION by F. H. Ludlow, p/c Graduate Council of Union College, Schenectady, NY

OH BRING HOME THE WAGON, JOHN (also titled OH BRING THE WAGON HOME, JOHN), no w/m credit given [arr. in CARMINA PRINCETONIA by Ernest Carter '88] p/c G. Schirmer, Inc.

OH BRING THE WAGON HOME, JOHN see Oh Bring Home the Wagon, John

OH, DIDN'T HE RAMBLE by Bob Cole and J. Rosamond Johnson, p/c Jos. W. Stern [1902]

OKLAHOMA!, (Tune from the musical *Oklahoma!*), by Oscar Hammerstein (w) and Richard Rodgers (m), p/c Williamson Music, Inc. (Theodore Presser and Co.)

THE OLD GREY MARE by Frank Panella (m), p/c Panella Music Co. [1915], assigned to Joe Morris Music Co. [1917], Joe Morris Music Co. (c) [1917]; assigned to Edwin H. Morris & Co.

OLD NASSAU by H. P. Peck (w) and Carl Langlotz (m), p/c PD

THE OLD OAKEN BUCKET by Samuel Woodworth (w) (Tune, JESSIE, THE FLOWER OF DUMBLANE), no composer credit given), p/c C. Bradlee, Boston [1833]. The words by Samuel Woodworth are now set to the tune of ARABY'S DAUGHTER by George Kiallmark.

OLD 124TH Geneva Psalter [1551]

ON BRAVE OLD ARMY TEAM by Enger, p/c Shapiro, Bernstein & Co.

ON, ON U OF K (University of Kentucky) By Carl A. Lampert, arr. W. Harry Clarke, p/c PD

ON PARADE by Edwin Franco Goldman, p/c Carl Fischer, Inc.

ON THE BANKS OF THE OLD RARITAN no w/m credit given, p/c PD

ON THE MALL by Edwin Franko Goldman (m), p/c Carl Fischer, Inc. [1923]

ON WINGS OF SONG by Heinrich Heine (German words) and Felix Mendelssohn (m) (original title AUF FLUGELN DES GESANGES), p/c Breitkopf & Hartel, Leipzig [1837]

ON WISCONSIN by Carl Beck (w) and W. T. Purdy (m), p/c Edwin H. Morris & Co.

ORANGE AND BLACK (refer to SADIE RAY)

OSTERREICHISCHE BUNDESHYMNE by W. A. Mozart (officially adopted as the Austrian anthem by the Austrian Cabinet on October 22, 1946), refer to NATIONAL ANTHEMS OF THE WORLD, edited by Martin Shaw and Henry Coleman, p/c Pitman Publishing Corp. [1960]. Most responses did not specify exact titles, and it is recommended that all national anthems be checked through the school in question because historical and political changes can present two or more options.

O TANNENBAUM (Tune, German folk song, also refer to MARYLAND! MY MARYLAND!)

OUR BOYS WILL SHINE TONIGHT or CENTRAL WILL SHINE TONIGHT no w/m credit given, p/c PD

OUR DIRECTOR MARCH by F. E. Bigelow, p/c Walter Jacobs, Inc. [1926] (Big 3 Music Corp.)

OUR HERITAGE MARCH by Karl L. King, p/c C. L. Barnhouse Co.

PERUNA (refer to COMING AROUND THE MOUNTAIN)

THE PIRATES CHORUS by Michael Balfe, p/c Edwin H. Morris & Co.

POMP AND CIRCUMSTANCE (also, LAND OF HOPE AND GLORY) by Edward Elgar, p/c Boosey & Co., London [1902]

PONY BATTLE CRY by James Dreibrodt, p/c Oz Music Publishers

THE POPE (also THE POPE, HE LEADS A MERRY LIFE) no w/m music credit given, traditional, p/c Osbourn's Music Saloon, Philadelphia [before 1842] PD

PRAYER OF THANKSGIVING (Tune, DANKGEBET), no (m) credit given, p/c G. Schirmer, Inc. [1894]

THE PRINCETON CANNON SONG MARCH by Hewitt and Osborne, p/c John Church Co. [1906], J. F. Hewitt and A. H. Osborn [1934], assigned to Shapiro, Bernstein & Co., Inc. [1934]

PRINCETON TRIANGLE CLUB SHOW p/c John Church Co., and the Princeton Triangle Club (Theodore Presser Co.)

PUT ON YOUR OLD GRAY BONNET by Stanley Murphy (w) and Percy Wenrich (m), p/c Jerome H. Remick & Co. [1909] (Warner Bros.)

QUAECUMQUE SUNT VERA by Joseph Haydn, p/c PD

THE RAMBLIN' WRECK FROM GEORGIA TECH by Frank Roman, p/c Frank Roman (Edwin H. Morris & Co.)

THE RED AND BLUE by W. J. Goeckel, p/c Associated Music Publishers, Inc. (Thornton W. Allen)

ROAR, ROAR LION, ROAR by Roy Webb and Morris W. Watkins, p/c Alumni Federation of Columbia University

RUSSIAN FOLK SONGS by A. Liadov (no other identification indicated), suggest individual contact with the school, also refer to NATIONAL ANTHEMS OF THE WORLD, edited by Martin Shaw and Henry Coleman, p/c Pitman Publishing Corp. [1960]. Most responses did not specify exact titles, and it is recommended that all national anthems be checked through the school in question because historical and political changes can present two or more options.

RUSSIAN NATIONAL ANTHEM could be one of three Russian anthems, THE CZARIST NATIONAL ANTHEM, THE INTERNATIONAL, and the UNION OF SOVIET SOCIALIST REPUBLICS, which replaced the others in [1943], no identification given by the schools, please contact them directly, also refer to NATIONAL ANTHEMS OF THE WORLD, edited by Martin Shaw and Henry Coleman, p/c Pitman Publishing Corp. [1968]. Most responses did not specify exact titles, and it is recommended that all national anthems be checked through the school in question because historical and political changes can present two or more options

SADIE RAY by J. Tannenbaum, p/c (ca. 1870) PD

ST. ANNE by Issac Watts [1674–1748] (w) and William Croft [1678–1727] (m), p/c PD

SAINTS IN CONCERT arr. William Moffit, p/c Hal Leonard Publishing Corp.

SCOTLAND THE BRAVE (also refer to MY BONNIE LASSIE), no w/m credit given, p/c Boosey & Hawkes, Inc.

SEMPER PARATUS [U.S. COAST GUARD SONG] by Francis Saltus Van

Boskerek, U.S.C.G. p/c Sam Fox Publishing Co., *U.S. Coast Guard Magazine* [1928], assigned to Sam Fox Publishing Co. [1938]

SOLOMON LEVI by Fred Seever, p/c PD

SONG OF THE VAGABONDS from "The Vagabond King" by Brian Hooker (w) and Rudolf Friml (m), p/c Henry Waterson, Inc. [1925]

SONGS OF BROWN UNIVERSITY, p/c Brown University, Providence R.I.

SONGS OF COLGATE p/c Broadcast Music, Inc. in cooperation with the Colgate University Alumni Association [1958]

SONGS OF JUNIATA (Jubilee Edition), p/c Hinds, Hayden & Eldredge, Inc. [1926] Huntingdon, PA

SONGS OF MARIETTA COLLEGE, p/c Marietta College

SONGS OF OBERLIN by Carolyn Rabson (editor), p/c Oberlin College Conservatory Library Oberlin, OH 44074

SONGS OF ROCKFORD COLLEGE [1954], p/c Rockford College, Rockford, IL

SONGS OF VILLANOVA COLLEGE arr. Paul Yoder, p/c J.W. Pepper & Son

SPANISH HYMN from WARTBURG COLLEGE HYMN BOOK, p/c Wartburg College, Waverly IA

THE SPIRIT OF INDEPENDENCE by Abe Holzmann (m), p/c Jerome H. Remick & Co. [1912]

STAND UP AND CHEER (used by University of Kansas) by Bowles, arr. Gori, p/c Edwin H. Morris & Co.

STAND UP AND CHEER (used by Juniata College) arr. E. Breitenfeld, p/c Hinds, Hayden & Eldredge, Inc

STAND UP AND CHEER (from film of same name) by Lew Brown (w) and Harry Akst (m), p/c Sam Fox Publishing Co., Cleveland, Movietone Music (c) [1934]

STAND UP AND CHEER (used by Baptist College, Charleston, SC) by Steve Rich (m), arr. Steve Rich, p/c not listed

THE STARS AND STRIPES FOREVER by John Philip Sousa, p/c John Church Co., Cincinnati [1897] (Theodore Presser, Inc.)

THE STEIN SONG by Lincoln Colcord and E. A. Fenstad, p/c Carl Fischer, Inc.

STEP TO THE REAR by Carolyn Leigh (w) and Elmer Bernstein (m), p/c Carwin Music, Inc.

THERE'LL ALWAYS BE AN ENGLAND by Ross Parker (w) and Michael Carr (m), p/c Shapiro, Bernstein & Co., Inc. [1939]

THERE'S MUSIC IN THE AIR by Frances Jane Crosby (Mrs. Alexander Van Alstyne) (w) and George Frederick Root (m), p/c William Hall & Son [1854]

TIGER RAG by Original Dixieland Jazz Band (m), p/c Leo Feist, Inc. [1917]

TILL WE MEET AGAIN by Raymond B. Egan (w) and Richard A. Whiting (m), p/c Jerome H. Remick & Co. [1918]

TRAMP! TRAMP! TRAMP! by George Frederick Root, p/c Root & Cady, Chicago [1864]

TRUE BLUE by Karl L. King, p/c Karl L. King Music House

UNITED STATES FIELD ARTILLERY MARCH by John Philip Sousa, p/c Carl Fischer, Inc. [1918]

UNIVERSITY OF MINNESOTA ROUSER (refer to MINNESOTA ROUSER)
UNIVERSITY OF NEW HAMPSHIRE SONG BOOK, p/c E. C. Schirmer Music Co., Boston MA
THE UNIVERSITY OF PENNSYLVANIA BAND MARCH or U OF P MARCH by Roland Seitz, p/c Roland F. Seitz
THE VICTORS by Louis Elbel, p/c Edwin H. Morris & Co.
THE WASHINGTON AND LEE SWING by C. A. Robbins (w) and Thornton W. Allen and M. W. Sheafe (m), p/c Thornton W. Allen [1910], Thornton W. Allen and R. G. Thach [1920], Thornton W. Allen [1930]
THE WATCH ON THE RHEIN (refer to DIE WACHT AM RHEIN)
WAVE THE FLAG by Gordon Erickson, p/c Edwin H. Morris & Co.
WEARING OF THE GREEN (Tune, of Irish origin and the words adapted to a traditional tune) [ca. 1797]
WE PRAISE THEE, O GOD by Croft, harmonized by G. F. Handel, p/c PD
WHEN IRISH EYES ARE SMILING by Chauncy Olcott and George Graff, Jr. (w) and Ernest R. Ball (m), p/c M. Witmark & Sons Co. [1912]
WHEN THE SAINTS GO MARCHING IN no w/m credit given, traditional, p/c PD
WHERE, O WHERE HAS MY LITTLE DOG GONE? (Tune, a German folk song, ZU LAUTERBACH HAB' I MEIN STRUMPF VERLOR'N), also known as DER DIETSCHER'S DOG by Septgimus Winner (w), p/c Sep. Winner & Co., Philadelphia [1864] PD
WHIFFENPOOF SONG [Yale University] by Guy H. Scull [1893–1894], adapted by Meade Minnigerode (w) and Tod B. Galloway (m), revised by Rudy Vallee and published by Miller Music Corp. [1936] (Big 3 Music Corp.)
WIN FOR AKRON by Dilley, arr. Jackoboice, p/c not listed
WINTERGREEN FOR PRESIDENT (OF THEE I SING) by Ira Gershwin (w) and George Gershwin (m), p/c New World Music Corp. [1923]
YALE BOOLA by A. M. Hirsch, p/c PD
YALE SONG BOOK, p/c Yale University, New Haven CT
THE YELLOW AND BLUE by Charles M. Gayley (w) and Michael William Balfe (m), p/c PD

School Names

Abilene Christian University, Abilene, TX
Adelphi University, Garden City, NY
Adirondack Community College, Glens Falls, NY
Adrian College, Adrian, MI
Alabama A & M University, Normal, AL
Alabama State University, Montgomery, AL
Alaska Methodist University, Anchorage, AK
Alaska Pacific University, Anchorage, AK
Albion College, Albion, MI
Albright College, Reading, PA
Alice Lloyd College, Pippa Passes, KY
Allan Hancock College, Santa Maria, CA
Allegheny College, Meadville, PA
Alma College, Alma, MI
Alverno College, Milwaukee, WI
Amherst College, Amherst, MA
Anderson University, Anderson, IN
Andrews University, Berrien Springs, MI
Appalachian Bible Institute, Bradley, WV
Appalachian State University, Boone, NC
Aquinas College, Grand Rapids, MI
Arizona State University, Tempe, AZ
Arizona Western College, Yuma, AZ
Arkansas State University, Jonesboro, AR
Asbury College, Wilmore, KY
Ashland University, Ashland, OH
Assumption College, Worcester, MA
Atlanta University, Atlanta, GA
Atlantic Christian College, Wilson, NC

Auburn University, Auburn, AL
Augsburg College, Minneapolis, MN
Augusta College, Augusta, GA
Augustana College, Sioux Falls, SD
Aurora University, Aurora, IL
Austin College, Sherman, TX
Austin Peay State University, Clarksville, TN
Baker University, Baldwin City, KS
Baldwin-Wallace College, Berea, OH
Ball State University, Muncie, IN
Baptist College, Charleston, SC
Barber-Scotia College, Concord, NC
Barton County Community College, Great Bend, KS
Bates College, Lewiston, ME
Baylor University, Waco, TX
Bellarmine College, Louisville, KY
Belmont Abbey College, Belmont, NC
Belmont College, Nashville, TN
Beloit College, Beloit, WI
Bemidji State University, Bemidji, MN
Benedict College, Columbia, SC
Benedictine College, Atchison, KS
Bergen Community College, Paramus, NJ
Bernard M. Baruch College (CUNY), New York, NY
Bethany College, Bethany, WV
Bethany College, Lindsborg, KS
Bethel College, Mishawaka, IN
Bethel College, North Newton, KS
Bethel College, Saint Paul, MN
Bethune-Cookman College, Daytona Beach, FL
Big Bend Community College, Moses Lake, WA
Birmingham-Southern College, Birmingham, AL
Black Hawk College, Moline, IL
Bloomfield College, Bloomfield, NJ
Bloomsburg University of Pennsylvania, Bloomsburg, PA
Bluffton College, Bluffton, OH
Boston College, Chestnut Hill, MA
Boston University, Boston, MA
Bowdoin College, Brunswick, ME
Bowie State University, Bowie, MD
Bowling Green State University, Bowling Green, OH
Bradford College, Bradford, MA
Bradley University, Peoria, IL
Brandeis University, Waltham, MA
Briar Cliff College, Sioux City, IA
Bridgewater College, Bridgewater, VA
Brigham Young University, Laie, Oahu, HI
Brigham Young University, Provo, UT

Brooklyn College (CUNY), New York, NY
Brown University, Providence, RI
Bryant College, Smithfield, RI
Bryn Mawr College, Bryn Mawr, PA
Bucknell University, Lewisburg, PA
Buena Vista College, Storm Lake, IA
Butler University, Indianapolis, IN
Caldwell College, Caldwell, NJ
California Baptist College, Riverside, CA
California Institute of Technology, Pasadena, CA
California Lutheran University, Thousand Oaks. CA
California Polytechnic State University, San Luis Obispo, CA
California State Polytechnic University, Pomona, CA
California State University, Chico, CA
California State University, Dominguez Hills, CA
California State University, Fresno, CA
California State University, Fullerton, CA
California State University, Hayward, CA
California State University, Long Beach, CA
California State University, Los Angeles, CA
California State University, Northridge, CA
California State University, Sacramento, CA
California State University, San Jose, CA
California University of Pennsylvania, California, PA
Calvin College, Grand Rapids, MI
Cameron University, Lawton, OK
Canisius College, Buffalo, NY
Capital University, Columbus, OH
Carleton College, Northfield, MN
Carnegie Mellon University, Pittsburgh, PA
Carson-Newman College, Jefferson City, TN
Carthage College, Kenosha, WI
Case Western Reserve University, Cleveland, OH
Castleton State College, Castleton, VT
Catawba College, Salisbury, NC
Catholic University of America, Washington, DC
Central Arizona College, Coolidge, AZ
Central College of Iowa, Pella, IA
Central Connecticut State University, New Britain, CT
Central Florida Community College, Ocala, FL
Central Methodist College, Fayette, MO
Central Michigan University, Mt. Pleasant, MI
Central Missouri State University, Warrensburg, MO
Central State University, Edmond, OK
Central Washington University, Ellensburg, WA
Centre College, Danville, KY
Chadron State College, Chadron, NE
Chaminade University, Honolulu, HI

Chipola Junior College, Marianna, FL
City College (CUNY), New York, NY
Claflin College, Orangeburg, SC
Clarion University of Pennsylvania, Clarion, PA
Clarkson University, Potsdam, NY
Clark University, Worcester, MA
Clemson University, Clemson, SC
Coe College, Cedar Rapids, IA
Coker College, Hartsville, SC
Colby College, Waterville, ME
Colgate University, Hamilton, NY
College Misericordia, Dallas, PA
College of Charleston, Charleston, SC
College of Great Falls, Great Falls, MT
College of Notre Dame, Belmont, CA
College of Our Lady of the Elms, Chicopee, MA
College of St. Catherine, Saint Paul, MN
College of Saint Elizabeth, Convent Station, NJ
College of Saint Francis, Joliet, IL
College of Saint Scholastica, Duluth, MN
College of Saint Teresa, Winona, MN
College of Saint Thomas, Saint Paul, MN
College of Steubenville, Steubenville, OH
College of the Holy Cross, Worcester, MA
College of William and Mary, Williamsburg, VA
Colorado College, Colorado Springs, CO
Colorado State University, Fort Collins, CO
Columbia College, Columbia University, New York, NY
Community College of Allegheny County, Allegheny Campus, Pittsburgh, PA
Concord College, Athens, WV
Concordia College, Bronxville, NY
Concordia College, Moorhead, MN
Concordia College, Saint Paul, MN
Concordia Teachers College, Seward, NE
Connecticut College, New London, CT
Converse College, Spartanburg, SC
Coppin State College, Baltimore, MD
Cornell College, Mt. Vernon, IA
Cornell University, Ithaca, NY
Creighton University, Omaha, NE
Crowder College, Neosho, MO
C. S. Mott Community College, Flint, MI
Dakota State College, Madison, SD
Dakota Wesleyan University, Mitchell, SD
Dartmouth College, Hanover, NH
David Lipscomb University, Nashville, TN
Davidson College, Davidson, NC
Delta State University, Cleveland, MS

Denison University, Granville, OH
De Paul University, Chicago, IL
De Pauw University, Greencastle, IN
Dickinson State University, Dickinson, ND
Dr. Martin Luther College, New Ulm, MN
Drake University, Des Moines, IA
Drexel University, Philadelphia, PA
Drury College, Springfield, MO
Duke University, Durham, NC
Duquesne University, Pittsburgh, PA
East Carolina University, Greenville, NC
East Central Community College, Decatur, MS
East Central University, Ada, OK
Eastern Illinois University, Charleston, IL
Eastern Iowa Community College District, Clinton, IA
Eastern Kentucky University, Richmond, KY
Eastern Michigan University, Ypsilanti, MI
Eastern New Mexico University, Portales, NM
Eastern Oregon State College, La Grande, OR
Eastern Washington University, Cheney, WA
Eastern Wyoming College, Torrington, WY
East Mississippi Community College, Scooba, MS
East Stroudsburg University of Pennsylvania, East Stroudsburg, PA
East Texas Baptist University, Marshall, TX
East Texas State University, Commerce, TX
Edinboro University of Pennsylvania, Edinboro, PA
Edison Community College, Fort Myers, FL
El Camino College, via Torrance, CA
Elizabethtown College, Elizabethtown, PA
Ellsworth Community College, Iowa Falls, IA
Elmhurst College, Elmhurst, IL
Elmira College, Elmira, NY
Elon College, Elon College, NC
Emerson College, Boston, MA
Emory University, Atlanta, GA
Emporia State University, Emporia, KS
Erie Community College (City Campus), Buffalo, NY
Fairfield University, Fairfield, CT
Fairleigh Dickinson University, Florham-Madison, Rutherford, and Teaneck-
    Hackensack, NJ
Fairmont State College, Fairmont, WV
Fayetteville State University, Fayetteville, NC
Fergus Falls Community College, Fergus Falls, MN
Ferris State University, Big Rapids, MI
Fitchburg State College, Fitchburg, MA
Florida Agricultural and Mechanical University, Tallahassee, FL
Florida Atlantic University, Boca Raton, FL
Florida International University, Miami, FL

Florida Southern College, Lakeland, FL
Florida State University, Tallahassee, FL
Fontbonne College, St. Louis, MO
Fordham University, Bronx, NY
Fort Hays State University, Fort Hays, KS
Framingham State College, Framingham, MA
Franciscan University, Steubenville, OH
Franklin and Marshall College, Lancaster, PA
Free Will Baptist Bible College, Nashville, TN
Friends University, Wichita, KS
Frostburg State University, Frostburg, MD
Furman University, Greenville, SC
Gardner-Webb College, Boiling Springs, NC
General Motors Institute, Flint, MI
Geneva College, Beaver Falls, PA
George Fox College, Newberg, OR
Georgetown University, Washington, DC
George Washington University, Washington, DC
Georgia College, Milledgeville, GA
Georgia Institute of Technology, Atlanta, GA
Georgia Southern College, Statesboro, GA
Georgia State University, Atlanta, GA
Gettysburg College, Gettysburg, PA
Glendale Community College, Glendale, AZ
Gonzaga University, Spokane, WA
Gordon College, Wenham, MA
Grace Bible College, Grand Rapids, MI
Grace College of the Bible, Omaha, NE
Graceland College, Lamoni, IA
Grambling State University, Grambling, LA
Grand Valley State University, Allendale, MI
Greenville College, Greenville, IL
Grinnell College, Grinnell, IA
Grove City College, Grove City, PA
Guilford College, Greensboro, NC
Gustavus Adolphus College, St. Peter, MN
Hamline University, Saint Paul, MN
Hampden-Sydney College, Hampden-Sydney, VA
Hanover College, Hanover, IN
Harding University, Searcy, AR
Hardin-Simmons University, Abilene, TX
Harpur College of State University of New York, Binghamton, NY
Harvard and Radcliffe Colleges, Cambridge, MA
Hastings College, Hastings, NE
Haverford College, Haverford, PA
Heidelberg College, Tiffin, OH
Henderson State University, Arkadelphia, AR
Herbert H. Lehman College (CUNY), Bronx, NY

Hibbing Community College, Hibbing, MN
High Point College, High Point, NC
Hillsdale College, Hillsdale, MI
Hinds Community College, Raymond, MS
Hiram College, Hiram, OH
Hofstra University, Hempstead, NY
Hope College, Holland, MI
Howard Payne University, Brownwood, TX
Howard University, Washington, DC
Hunter College (CUNY), New York, NY
Huron University, Huron, SD
Idaho State University, Pocatello, ID
Illinois Benedictine College, Lisle, IL
Illinois Central College, East Peoria, IL
Illinois College, Jacksonville, IL
Illinois State University, Normal, IL
Illinois Wesleyan University, Bloomington, IL
Immaculata College, Immaculata, PA
Immaculata College of Washington, Washington, DC
Indiana State University, Terre Haute, IN
Indiana University, Bloomington, IN
Indiana University, South Bend, IN
Indiana University of Pennsylvania, Indiana, PA
Indiana University Southeast, New Albany, IN
Iona College, New Rochelle, NY
Iowa Lakes Community College, Estherville, IA
Iowa State University of Science and Technology, Ames, IA
Iowa Wesleyan College, Mount Pleasant, IA
Iowa Western Community College, Council Bluffs, IA
Ithaca College, Ithaca, NY
Jackson State University, Jackson, MS
Jacksonville State University, Jacksonville, AL
Jacksonville University, Jacksonville, FL
James Madison University, Harrisonburg, VA
Jamestown College, Jamestown, ND
Jersey City State College, Jersey City, NJ
John Carroll University, University Heights, OH
Johns Hopkins University, Baltimore, MD
Jones County Junior College, Ellisville, MS
Judson College, Marion, AL
Juniata College, Huntingdon, PA
Kalamazoo College, Kalamazoo, MI
Kansas State College, Pittsburg, KS
Kansas State University, Manhattan, KS
Kean College, Union, NJ
Kearney State College, Kearney, NE
Keene State College, Keene, NH
Kennesaw State College, Marietta, GA

Kent State University, Kent, OH
King's College, Wilkes-Barre, PA
Knox College, Galesburg, IL
Kutztown University of Pennsylvania, Kutztown, PA
Ladycliff College, Highland, NY
Lake Forest College, Lake Forest, IL
Lakeland College, Sheboygan, WI
Lake Superior State University, Sault Ste. Marie, MI
Lamar University, Beaumont, TX
Lane College, Jackson, TN
La Verne University, La Verne, CA
Lawrence Technological University, Southfield, MI
Lawrence University, Appleton, WI
Lebanon Valley College, Annville, PA
Lehigh University, Bethlehem, PA
Lenoir-Rhyne College, Hickory, NC
Limestone College, Gaffney, SC
Livingstone College, Salisbury, NC
Livingston University, Livingston, AL
Lock Haven University of Pennsylvania, Lock Haven, PA
Long Island University (Brooklyn Campus), Brooklyn, NY
Loras College, Dubuque, IA
Louisiana College, Pineville, LA
Louisiana State University and Agricultural and Mechanical College, Baton Rouge,
    LA
Louisiana Tech University, Ruston, LA
Loyola College, Baltimore, MD
Loyola University, Chicago, IL
Loyola University, New Orleans, LA
Luther College, Decorah, IA
Macalester College, Saint Paul, MN
McKendree College, Lebanon, IL
McMurry University, Abilene, TX
McNeese State University, Lake Charles, LA
Madonna College, Livonia, MI
Manchester College, North Manchester, IN
Manhattan College, Riverdale, NY
Manhattan (Borough of) Community College, New York, NY
Mankato State University, Mankato, MN
Mansfield University of Pennsylvania, Mansfield, PA
Marietta College, Marietta, OH
Marion College, Marion, IN
Marquette University, Milwaukee, WI
Marshalltown Community College, Iowa Valley Community College District,
    Marshalltown, IA
Marshall University, Huntington, WV
Mary, University of, Bismarck, ND
Marylhurst College for Lifelong Learning, Marylhurst, OR

Mary Manse College, Toledo, OH
Marymount College, Tarrytown, NY
Massachusetts Institute of Technology, Cambridge, MA
Massachusetts State College, Fitchburg, MA
Mayville State University, Mayville, ND
Memphis State University, Memphis, TN
Mercer County Community College, Trenton, NJ
Mercy College, Dobbs Ferry, NY
Meredith College, Raleigh, NC
Merrimack College, North Andover, MA
Mesa State College, Grand Junction, CO
Methodist College, Fayetteville, NC
Miami University, Oxford, OH
Michigan State University, East Lansing, MI
Michigan Technological University, Houghton, MI
Mid-America Nazarene College, Olathe, KS
Middle Tennessee State University, Murfreesboro, TN
Midwestern State University, Wichita Falls, TX
Millersville University of Pennsylvania, Millersville, PA
Milligan College, Milligan College, TN
Millikin University, Decatur, IL
Mills College, Oakland, CA
Minot State University, Minot, ND
Mississippi College, Clinton, MS
Mississippi Delta Community College, Moorhead, MS
Mississippi State University, State College, MS
Mississippi University for Women, Columbus, MS
Missouri Southern State College, Joplin, MO
Missouri Valley College, Marshall, MO
Missouri Western State College, St. Joseph, MO
Mobile College, Mobile, AL
Monmouth College, West Long Branch, NJ
Montana State University, Bozeman, MT
Montclair State College, Upper Montclair, NJ
Montgomery College, Rockville, MD
Moorhead State University, Moorhead, MN
Moravian College, Bethlehem, PA
Morehead State University, Morehead, KY
Morgan State University, Baltimore, MD
Morningside College, Sioux City, IA
Morris Brown College, Atlanta, GA
Mount Holyoke College, South Hadley, MA
Mount Mary College, Milwaukee, WI
Mount Mercy College, Cedar Rapids, IA
Mount Saint Mary's College and Seminary, Emmitsburg, MD
Mount St. Mary's College, Los Angeles, CA
Mount Union College, Alliance, OH
Muhlenberg College, Allentown, PA

Murray State University, Murray, KY
Muskingum College, New Concord, OH
Nazareth College, Rochester, NY
Nebraska Wesleyan University, Lincoln, NE
Newark State College, Union, NJ
New Jersey Institute of Technology, Newark, NJ
New Mexico Highlands University, Las Vegas, NM
New Mexico Military Institute, Roswell, NM
New Mexico State University, Las Cruces, NM
New York University, New York, NY
Niagara University, Niagara University, NY
Norfolk State University, Norfolk, VA
North Carolina Agricultural and Technical State University, Greensboro, NC
North Carolina State University, Raleigh, NC
North Dakota State University, Fargo, ND
Northeastern A & M College, Miami, OK
Northeastern Illinois University, Chicago, IL
Northeastern Oklahoma State University, Tahlequah, OK
Northeast Louisiana University, Monroe, LA
Northeast Missouri State University, Kirksville, MO
Northern Arizona University, Flagstaff, AZ
Northern Illinois University, De Kalb, IL
Northern Kentucky University, Highland Heights, KY
Northern Michigan University, Marquette, MI
Northern Montana College, Havre, MT
Northern State University, Aberdeen, SD
North Georgia College, Dahlonega, GA
North Iowa Area Community College, Mason City, IA
Northland Community College, Thief River Falls, MN
North Park College and Theological Seminary, Chicago, IL
North Texas State University, Denton, TX
Northwest Christian College, Eugene, OR
Northwest Community College, Powell, WY
Northwestern College, Orange City, IA
Northwestern College, Watertown, WI
Northwestern Oklahoma State University, Alva, OK
Northwestern State University, Natchitoches, LA
Northwestern University, Evanston, IL
Northwest Missouri State University, Maryville, MO
Northwest Nazarene College, Nampa, ID
Notre Dame College, Cleveland, OH
Oberlin College, Oberlin, OH
Odessa College, Odessa, TX
Ohio Northern University, Ada, OH
Ohio State University, Columbus, OH
Ohio University, Athens, OH
Oklahoma Baptist University, Shawnee, OK
Oklahoma Christian College, Oklahoma City, OK

Oklahoma City University, Oklahoma City, OK
Oklahoma State University, Stillwater, OK
Old Dominion University, Norfolk, VA
Olivet College, Olivet, MI
Olivet Nazarene University, Kankakee, IL
Orange Coast College, Costa Mesa, CA
Orange County Community College, Middletown, NY
Oral Roberts University, Tulsa, OK
Oregon College of Education, Monmouth, OR
Oregon State University, Corvallis, OR
Otterbein College, Westerville, OH
Ottumwa Heights College, Ottumwa, IA
Ouachita Baptist University, Arkadelphia, AR
Our Lady of the Lake College, San Antonio, TX
Pace University, New York, Pleasantville, White Plains, NY
Pacific Lutheran University, Tacoma, WA
Pacific Union College, Angwin, CA
Pacific University, Forest Grove, OR
Pan American University, Edinburg, TX
Panhandle State University, Goodwell, OK
Pennsylvania State University, University Park, PA
Pensacola Junior College, Pensacola, FL
Pfeiffer College, Misenheimer, NC
Phillips University, Enid, OK
Phoenix College, Phoenix, AZ
Pittsburg State University, Pittsburg, KS
Plymouth State College, Plymouth, NH
Polytechnic University, Brooklyn, NY
Portland State University, Portland, OR
Prairie View A & M University, Prairie View, TX
Presbyterian College, Clinton, SC
Presentation College, Aberdeen, SD
Princeton University, Princeton, NJ
Principia College, Elsah, IL
Providence College, Providence, RI
Purdue University, West Lafayette, IN
Queensborough Community College (CUNY), Bayside, NY
Queens College, Charlotte, NC
Quincy College, Quincy, IL
Quinnipiac College, Hamden, CT
Radcliffe College, Cambridge, MA (also refer to Harvard College)
Radford University, Radford, VA
Rainy River Community College, International Falls, MN
Ramapo College of New Jersey, Mahwah, NJ
Regis College, Weston, MA
Rensselaer Polytechnic Institute, Troy, NY
Rhode Island College, Providence, RI
Rhode Island Community College, Warwick, RI

Rice University, Houston, TX
Ricks College, Rexburg, ID
Rio Hondo College, Whittier, CA
Rivier College, Nashua, NH
Roanoke College, Salem, WV
Robert Morris College, Coraopolis, PA
Roberts Wesleyan College, Rochester, NY
Rochester Community College, Rochester, MN
Rochester Institute of Technology, Rochester, NY
Rockford College, Rockford, IL
Rocky Mountain College, Billings, MT
Rollins College, Winter Park, FL
Rose-Hulman Institute of Technology, Terre Haute, IN
Rutgers-University College, New Brunswick, NJ
Sacramento City College, Sacramento, CA
Sacramento State University, Sacramento, CA
Saddleback College, Mission Viejo, CA
Saginaw Valley State University, University Center, MI
St. Ambrose University, Davenport, IA
Saint Anselm College, Manchester, NH
Saint Augustine's College, Raleigh, NC
St. Bernard College, St. Bernard, AL
St. Cloud State University, St. Cloud, MN
St. Edward's University, Austin, TX
Saint Francis College, Loretto, PA
St. John's College, Annapolis, MD
St. John's University, Collegeville, MN
St. John's University, Jamaica, NY
Saint Joseph's College, Rensselaer, IN
St. Lawrence University, Canton, NY
Saint Leo College, Saint Leo, FL
St. Louis University, St. Louis, MO
Saint Mary College, Leavenworth, KS
St. Mary of the Plains College, Dodge City, KS
Saint Mary-of-the-Woods College, Saint Mary-of-the-Woods, IN
Saint Mary's College, Notre Dame, IN
Saint Mary's College of Maryland, St. Mary's City, MD
St. Mary's Dominican College, New Orleans, LA
St. Norbert College, De Pere, WI
St. Olaf College, Northfield, MN
Saint Peter's College, Jersey City, NJ
St. Procopius College, Lisle, IL
St. Vincent College and Seminary, Latrobe, PA
Salem State College, Salem, MA
Salem-Teikyo University, Salem, WV
Salisbury State University, Salisbury, MD
Salve Regina, the Newport College, Newport, RI
Samford University, Birmingham, AL

Sam Houston State University, Huntsville, TX
San Diego State University, San Diego, CA
San Francisco State University, San Francisco, CA
San Jacinto State College, Pasadena, TX
San Jose State University, San Jose, CA
School of the Ozarks, Point Lookout, MO
Schoolcraft College, Livonia, MI
Seattle Pacific University, Seattle, WA
Seton Hall University, South Orange, NJ
Seton Hill College, Greensburg, PA
Shaw University, Raleigh, NC
Sheldon Jackson College, Sitka, AK
Shenandoah College and Conservatory of Music, Winchester, VA
Shepherd College, Shepherdstown, WV
Shippensburg University of Pennsylvania, Shippensburg, PA
Simpson College, Indianola, IA
Sioux Empire College, Hawarden, IA
Sioux Falls College, Sioux Falls, SD
Slippery Rock University of Pennsylvania, Slippery Rock, PA
Smith College, Northampton, MA
South Carolina State College, Orangeburg, SC
South Dakota School of Mines and Technology, Rapid City, SD
South Dakota State University, Brookings, SD
Southeastern Louisiana University, Hammond, LA
Southeastern Massachusetts University, North Dartmouth, MA
Southeastern Olkahoma State University, Durant, OK
Southeast Missouri State University, Cape Girardeau, MO
Southern Baptist College, Walnut Ridge, AR
Southern College of Seventh-Day Adventists, Collegedale, TN
Southern Colorado State College, Pueblo, CO
Southern Connecticut State University, New Haven, CT
Southern Illinois University, Carbondale, IL
Southern Methodist University, Dallas, TX
Southern Oregon State College, Ashland, OR
Southern State, Springfield, SD
Southern University and A & M College, Baton Rouge, LA
Southwestern at Memphis, Memphis, TN
Southwestern College, Winfield, KS
Southwestern Oklahoma State University, Weatherford, OK
Southwestern Oregon Community College, Coos Bay, OR
Southwestern University, Georgetown, TX
Southwest State University, Marshall, MN
Southwest Missouri State University, Springfield, MO
Southwest Texas State University, San Marcos, TX
Springfield College, Springfield, MA
Spring Hill College, Mobile, AL
Stanford University, Stanford, CA
State University of New York (SUNY), Albany, NY

State University of New York College, Brockport, NY
State University of New York College, Buffalo, NY
State University of New York College, Cortland, NY
State University of New York College, Fredonia, NY
State University of New York College, Geneseo, NY
State University of New York College, New Paltz, NY
State University of New York College, Stony Brook, NY
State University of New York College of Agriculture & Technology, Cobleskill, NY
Stephen F. Austin State University, Nacogdoches, TX
Sterling College, Sterling, KS
Stetson University, DeLand, FL
Stillman College, Tuscaloosa, AL
Swarthmore College, Swarthmore, PA
Syracuse University, Syracuse, NY
Tabor College, Hillsboro, KS
Talladega College, Talladega, AL
Tarleton State University, Stephenville, TX
Taylor University, Upland, IN
Temple University, Philadelphia, PA
Tennessee State University, Nashville, TN
Tennessee Technological University, Cookeville, TN
Tennessee Temple University, Chattanooga, TN
Tennessee Wesleyan College, Athens, TN
Texas A & I University, Kingsville, TX
Texas A & M University, College Station, TX
Texas Christian University, Fort Worth, TX
Texas Southern University, Houston, TX
Texas Tech University, Lubbock, TX
Texas Woman's University, Denton, TX
Tougaloo College, Tougaloo, MS
Towson State University, Baltimore, MD
Transylvania University, Lexington, KY
Trenton State College, Trenton, NJ
Trinity College, Hartford, CT
Troy State University, Troy, AL
Tufts University, Medford, MA
Tulane University, New Orleans, LA
Tuskegee University, Tuskegee, AL
Union College, Barbourville, KY
Union College, Lincoln, NE
Union College, Schenectady, NY
Union University, Jackson, TN
United States Air Force Academy, Colorado Springs, CO
United States Coast Guard Academy, New London, CT
United States Military Academy (Army), West Point, NY
United States Naval Academy, Annapolis, MD
University of Akron, Akron, OH

University of Alabama, Birmingham, AL
University of Alabama, Montevallo, AL
University of Alabama, Tuscaloosa, AL
University of Alaska, Anchorage, AK
University of Alaska, Fairbanks, AK
University of Arizona, Tucson, AZ
University of Arkansas, Fayetteville, AR
University of Arkansas, Little Rock, AR
University of Arkansas, Monticello, AR
University of Arkansas, Pine Bluff, AR
University of Bridgeport, Bridgeport, CT
University of California, Berkeley, CA
University of California, Davis, CA
University of California (UCLA), Los Angeles, CA
University of California, Santa Barbara, CA
University of California, Santa Cruz, CA
University of Central Arkansas, Conway, AR
University of Chicago, Chicago, IL
University of Cincinnati, Cincinnati, OH
University of Colorado, Boulder, CO
University of Colorado, Denver, CO
University of Connecticut, Storrs, CT
University of Dayton, Dayton, OH
University of Delaware, Newark, DE
University of Denver, Denver, CO
University of Detroit, Detroit, MI
University of Dubuque, Dubuque, IA
University of Evansville, Evansville, IN
University of Findlay, Findlay, OH
University of Florida, Gainesville, FL
University of Georgia, Athens, GA
University of Hartford, West Hartford, CT
University of Hawaii, Hilo, HI
University of Hawaii, Honolulu, HI
University of Hawaii at Manoa, Honolulu, HI
University of Houston (Downtown), Houston, TX
University of Houston (University Park), Houston, TX
University of Idaho, Moscow, ID
University of Illinois, Urbana/Champaign, IL
University of Iowa, Iowa City, IA
University of Kansas, Lawrence, KS
University of Kentucky, Lexington, KY
University of Louisville, Louisville, KY
University of Maine, Fort Kent, ME
University of Maine, Orono, ME
University of Mary Hardin-Baylor, Belton, TX
University of Maryland, College Park, MD
University of Maryland/Eastern Shore, Princess Ann, MD

University of Massachusetts, Amherst, MA
University of Miami, Coral Gables, FL
University of Michigan, Ann Arbor, MI
University of Minnesota, Crookston, MN
University of Minnesota, Minneapolis, MN
University of Mississippi, Oxford, MS
University of Mississippi, University, MS
University of Missouri, Columbia, MO
University of Missouri, Kansas City, MO
University of Missouri, Rolla, MO
University of Montana, Missoula, MT
University of Nebraska, Lincoln, NE
University of Nebraska, Omaha, NE
University of Nevada, Las Vegas, NV
University of Nevada, Reno, NV
University of New Hampshire, Durham, NH
University of New Haven, West Haven, CT
University of New Mexico, Albuquerque, NM
University of New Orleans, New Orleans, LA
University of North Alabama, Florence, AL
University of North Carolina, Asheville, NC
University of North Carolina, Chapel Hill, NC
University of North Carolina, Greensboro, NC
University of North Carolina, Wilmington, NC
University of North Dakota (Lake Region), Devil's Lake, ND
University of North Dakota, Grand Forks, ND
University of Northern Colorado, Greeley, CO
University of Northern Iowa, Cedar Falls, IA
University of North Texas, Denison, TX
University of Notre Dame, Notre Dame, IN
University of Oklahoma, Norman, OK
University of Oregon, Eugene, OR
University of Pennsylvania, Philadelphia, PA
University of Pittsburgh, Pittsburgh, PA
University of Portland, Portland, OR
University of Puget Sound, Tacoma, WA
University of Rhode Island, Kingston, RI
University of Richmond, Richmond, VA
University of Rochester, Rochester, NY
University of South Carolina, Columbia, SC
University of South Dakota, Vermillion, SD
University of Southern California, Los Angeles, CA
University of Southern Colorado, Pueblo, CO
University of Southern Indiana, Evansville, IN
University of Southern Mississippi, Hattiesburg, MS
University of South Florida, Tampa, FL
University of Southwestern Louisiana, Lafayette, LA
University of Tennessee, Chattanooga, TN

University of Tennessee, Knoxville, TN
University of Texas, Arlington, TX
University of Texas, Austin, TX
University of Texas, El Paso, TX
University of Texas, San Antonio, TX
University of the Ozarks, Clarksville, AR
University of the Pacific, Stockton, CA
University of Toledo, Toledo, OH
University of Tulsa, Tulsa, OK
University of Utah, Salt Lake City, UT
University of Vermont, Burlington, VT
University of Virginia, Charlottesville, VA
University of Washington, Seattle, WA
University of Wisconsin, Eau Claire, WI
University of Wisconsin, Green Bay, WI
University of Wisconsin, La Crosse, WI
University of Wisconsin, Madison, WI
University of Wisconsin, Milwaukee, WI
University of Wisconsin, Oshkosh, WI
University of Wisconsin, Parkside, WI
University of Wisconsin, Platteville, WI
University of Wisconsin, River Falls, WI
University of Wisconsin, Stevens Point, WI
University of Wisconsin/Stout, Menomonie, WI
University of Wisconsin, Superior, WI
University of Wisconsin, Whitewater, WI
University of Wyoming, Laramie, WY
Upper Iowa University, Fayette, IA
Upsala College, East Orange, NJ
Ursuline College, Pepper Pike, OH
Utah State University, Logan, UT
Valdosta State College, Valdosta, GA
Valley City State University, Valley City, ND
Valparaiso University, Valparaiso, IN
Vanderbilt University, Nashville, TN
Vassar College, Poughkeepsie, NY
Vennard College, University Park, IA
Vermont Technical College, Randolph Center, VT
Villanova University, Villanova, PA
Virginia Polytechnic Institute and State University, Blacksburg, VA
Virginia State University, Petersburg, VA
Viterbo College, La Crosse, WI
Wake Forest University, Winston-Salem, NC
Waldorf College, Forest City, IA
Walker College, Jasper, AL
Walla Walla College, College Place, WA
Wartburg College, Waverly, IA
Washburn University, Topeka, KS

Washington and Jefferson College, Washington, PA
Washington and Lee University, Lexington, VA
Washington State University, Pullman, WA
Washington University, St. Louis, MO
Waubonsee College, Sugar Grove, IL
Wayne State College, Wayne, NE
Wayne State University, Detroit, MI
Waynesburg College, Waynesburg, PA
Weber State College, Ogden, UT
Webster University, St. Louis, MO
Wellesley College, Wellesley, MA
Wentworth Military Academy and Junior College, Lexington, MO
Wesleyan College, Macon, GA
West Chester University of Pennsylvania, West Chester, PA
Western Carolina University, Cullowhee, NC
Western Illinois University, Macomb, IL
Western Kentucky University, Bowling Green, KY
Western Michigan University, Kalamazoo, MI
Western Montana College of the University of Montana, Dillon, MT
Western New England College, Springfield, MA
Western New Mexico University, Silver City, NM
Western State College of Colorado, Gunnison, CO
Western Washington University, Bellingham, WA
Westfield State College, Westfield, MA
West Georgia College, Carrollton, GA
West Liberty State College, West Liberty, WV
Westmar College, Le Mars, IA
Westminster College, Florence, MS
Westminster College, Fulton, MO
Westminster College, New Wilmington, PA
West Texas State University, Canyon, TX
West Virginia Institute of Technology, Montgomery, WV
West Virginia State College, Institute, WV
West Virginia University, Morgantown, WV
West Virginia Wesleyan College, Buckhannon, WV
Wheaton College, Wheaton, IL
Wheeling Jesuit College, Wheeling, WV
Wheelock College, Boston, MA
Whitman College, Walla Walla, WA
Whittier College, Whittier, CA
Wichita State University, Wichita, KS
Wilkes University, Wilkes-Barre, PA
Willamette University, Salem, OR
William Carey College, Hattiesburg, MS
William Jewell College, Liberty, MO
William Paterson College, Wayne, NJ
William Penn College, Oskaloosa, IA
Williams College, Williamstown, MA

Willmar Community College, Willmar, MN
Wingate College, Wingate, NC
Winona State University, Winona, MN
Winthrop College, Rock Hill, SC
Wisconsin, University of La Crosse, WI
Wittenberg University, Springfield, OH
Wofford College, Spartanburg, SC
Worcester Polytechnic Institute, Worcester, MA
Worcester State College, Worcester, MA
Wright State University, Dayton, OH
Xavier University, Cincinnati, OH
Yale University, West Haven, CT
Yavapai College, Prescott, AZ
York College of Pennsylvania, York, PA
Youngstown State University, Youngstown, OH

References

AMERICAN COLLEGE REGALIA: A HANDBOOK compiled by Linda Sparks and Bruce Emerton, published by Greenwood Press, Westport, CT 06881 [1988]

BAND MUSIC GUIDE published by Instrumentalist Co., Evanston, IL 60204 [1975]

BAND MUSIC GUIDE ADDENDUM published by Instrumentalist Co., Evanston, IL 60204 [1975]

BARRON'S PROFILES OF AMERICAN COLLEGES published by Barron's Educational Series, Inc., New York, NY [1990]

CARMINA PRINCETONIA (The Song Book of Princeton University) edited by a university committee with biographical sketches of alumni authors and composers, published by G. Schirmer, Inc., New York, NY [1968]

COLLEGE SONGS ON PARADE published by Edwin H. Morris & Co., New York, NY [1970]

THE GOLDEN BOOK OF FAVORITE SONGS compiled and edited by John W. Beattie, William Breach, Mabelle Glenn, Walter J. Goodell, Edgar B. Gordon, Norman H. Hall, Ernest G. Hesser, and E. Jane Wisenall, published by Hall & McCreary Company, Chicago, IL [1946]

HALLELUJAH TROMBONE! by Paul E. Bierley, published by Integrity Press, Columbus, OH [1982]

INTERCOLLEGIATE SONG BOOK compiled by Thornton W. Allen and edited by Carl F. Price, p/c Intercollegiate Song Book, Inc. (Theodore W. Allen Company) New York, NY [1931]

INTERNATIONAL SONG BOOK published by M. M. Cole Publishing Co., 251 E. Grand Avenue, Chicago, IL 60611 [1933]

JASS GUIDE TO P. D. MUSIC compiled and edited by Jules Russell, published by Jass Enterprises, New York, NY 10017 [1966]

LET VOICES RING compiled and arranged by Ruth Heller and Walter Goodell, published by Hall & McCreary Company, Chicago, IL [1949]

THE MUSIC OF HENRY FILLMORE AND WILL HUFF by Paul E. Bierely, published by Integrity Press, Columbus, OH [1982]

NATIONAL ANTHEMS OF THE WORLD edited by Martin Shaw and Henry Coleman, published by Pitman Publishing Corp., New York, NY/London [1960]

SONG DEX TREASURY OF WORLD FAMOUS INSTRUMENTAL MUSIC compiled and edited by George Goodwin, published by Song Dex, Inc., New York, NY [1955]

SONGS WE SING edited and arranged by Fowler Smith, Hartry Robert Wilson and Glenn H. Woods, published by Hall & McCreary Company, Chicago, IL [1940–1941]

SWEET AND LOWDOWN (America's Popular Song Writers) by Warren Craig with Foreword by Milton Ager, published by Scarecrow Press, Inc., Metuchen, New York, and London [1978]

VARIETY MUSIC CAVALCADE [1920–1961] by Julius Mattfeld, published by Prentice-Hall, Inc., Englewood Cliffs, NJ [1962]

THE WORKS OF JOHN PHILIP SOUSA by Paul E. Bierley, published by Integrity Press, Columbus, OH 43219-3013 [1984]

THE WORLD'S MOST BELOVED HUMOROUS AND NOSTALGIC SONGS (Part One) compiled and edited by George Goodwin, published by Song Dex, Inc., Box 49, New York, NY [1956]

THE WORLD'S MOST BELOVED HUMOROUS AND NOSTALGIC SONGS (Part Two) compiled and edited by George Goodwin, published by Song Dex, Inc., Box 49, New York, NY [1963]

Publisher

Allen Intercollegiate Music, Inc. (refer to Associated Music Publishers, Inc.)
Thornton W. Allen (refer to Associated Music Publishers, Inc.)
Ashley Publications, Inc., 133 Industrial Ave. (Box 337), Hasbrouck Heights, NJ 07604
Associated Music Publishers, Inc., 866 Third Ave. New York, NY 10022
C. L Barnhouse, Box 680, Oskaloosa, IA 52577
Belwin/Mills Publishing Corp., Columbia Plaza, East, Burbank, CA 91505
Benson Publishing Group, 365 Great Cir., Nashville, TN 37228
Big 3 Music Corp., 729 Seventh Ave., New York, NY 10019 (see Columbia Pictures Publications)
Boosey and Co. (refer to Boosey and Hawkes, Inc.)
Boosey and Hawkes, Inc., 24 W. 57th St., New York, NY 10019
George F. Briegel, Inc., 4 Summit Ct., Flushing, NY 11355
Broadcast Music, Inc., 320 West 57th St., New York, NY 10019
Brodt Music Co., PO Box 1207, Charlotte, NC 28201
Alexander Broude, Inc. 225 W. 57th St., New York, NY 10019
Broude Bros., 56 W. 45th St., New York, NY 10036
Carwin Music, Inc., 31 W. 54th Street, New York, NY 10019
Chappell and Co., Ltd., 810 Seventh Ave., New York, NY 10019
John Church Co. (refer to Theodore Presser Co.)
John Church, Jr. (refer to Theodore Presser Co.)
M. M. Cole Publishing Co., 251 E. Grand Ave., Chicago, IL 60611
Columbia Pictures Publications, 15800 NW 48th Ave., Miami, FL 33014
Oliver Ditson and Co. (refer to Theodore Presser Co.)
Elkan-Vogel (refer to Theodore Presser Co.)
Leo Feist, Inc. (refer to Big 3 Music Corp.—see Columbia Pictures Publications)
Fillmore Music House (refer to Carl Fischer, Inc.)
Carl Fischer, Inc., 62 Cooper Square, New York, NY 10003

Sam Fox Publishing Co., Inc., 313B, E. Plaza Drive, Suite 13, Santa Maria, CA 93454

Hansen Publications, 1860 Broadway, New York, NY 10023

Hawkes and Son, Ltd. (refer to Boosey and Hawkes, Inc.)

Ralph Hermann (refer to Podium Music, Inc.)

House of Bryant Publications, 530 West Main Street, Hendersonville, TN 37075

Walter Jacobs, Inc. (refer Big 3 Music Corp.—see Columbia Pictures Publications)

Karl L. King Music House (K. L. King Music Publications) (refer to C. L. Barnhouse Co.)

Neil A. Kjos Music Company, 4382 Jutland Dr., San Diego, CA 92117

Hal Leonard Publishing Corp., 8112 Bluemound Rd., Milwaukee, WI 53213

Loop Publishing Co. (refer to Neil A. Kjos Music Company)

MCA Music, 70 Universal City Plaza—Los Angeles, CA 91608

Melrose Music Corp. (see Hanson Publications—see Edwin H. Morris and Co., Inc.—refer to Hal Leonard Publishing Corp.)

Miller Music Corp. (refer to Big 3 Music Corp.—see Columbia Pictures Publications)

Edwin H. Morris and Co., Inc., 39 West 54th St., New York, NY 10019 (see Hansen Publications—also refer to Hal Leonard Publishing Corp.)

The Music Shop, Minneapolis, MN

New World Music Co., Ltd. (refer to Warner Bros. Music)

Oz Music Publishers, 6875 El Cajon Blvd., San Diego, CA 92115

Panella Music Co., 25 Seneca Rd., Pittsburgh, PA 15241

Paragon Associates, Inc., P.O. Box 23618, Nashville, TN 37202

Paragon Music Co. (refer to Ashley Publications, Inc.)

Paragon Music Corp. (refer to the Benson Publishing Group)

Peer-Southern Organization, 1740 Broadway, New York, NY 10019

J. W. Pepper and Son, 2480 Industrial Drive, Paloi, PA 19301

Pitman Publishing Corp., New York, NY/London

Plymouth Music Co., Inc., 170 NE 33rd St., Fort Lauderdale, FL 33334

Podium Music, Inc., 4 Broadway, Valhalla, NY 10595

Theodore Presser Co., Presser Place, Bryn Mawr, PA 19010

Remick Music Corp. (refer to Warner Bros. Music)

Jerome H. Remick and Co. (refer to Warner Bros. Publications)

The Richmond Organization, 17 W. 60th St., New York, NY 10023

Robbins Music Corp. (refer to Big 3 Music Corp.—see Columbia Pictures Publications)

Rubank, Inc., 16215 NW 15th Ave., Miami, FL 33169

E. C. Schirmer Music, 112 South St., Boston, MA 02111

G. Schirmer, Inc., 866 3rd Ave., New York, NY 10022

Select Music Publications, Inc. 1619 Broadway, New York, NY 10019

Shapiro, Bernstein and Co., Inc., 10 East 53rd St., 19th floor, New York, NY 10022

Southern Music Co., 1100 Broadway, San Antonio, TX 78292

Southern Music Publishing Co., Inc. (refer to Peer-Southern Organization)

Sweet Music, Inc., 1216 Meadowbrook Rd., Altadena, CA 91001

George V. Thompson, Ltd., Toronto, Canada

Warner Bros. Music, 9000 Sunset Blvd., Los Angeles, CA 90069
Warner Bros. Publications, 75 Rockefeller Plaza, New York, NY 10019
White-Smith Publishing Co. (check with the music department of school providing publisher information)
Williamson Music, Inc. (refer to Chappell and Co., Ltd.)
M. Witmark and Sons, Co. (refer to Warner Bros. Publications)
Words and Music, Inc. (check with the music department of school providing publisher information)

OTHER PUBLISHERS

Ascherberg, Hopwood and Crews, Ltd. [1917], London
F. D. Benteen [1851], Baltimore, MD
C. Bradlee [1833], Boston, MA
Breitkopf and Hartel [1911], Leipzig
Draper and Folsom [1778], Boston, MA
Feist and Frankenthaler [1901]
B. Feldman and Co. [1912]
Firth, Pond and Co. [1860]
Joseph H. Flanner [1910]
Flanner-Hafsoos Music House [1909]
William Hall and Son [1854]
James L. Hewitt & Co. [1826], Boston, MA
Higgins Bros. [1857], Chicago, IL
Hinds, Hayden and Eldredge, Inc. [1926], Huntingdon, PA
Miller and Beacham [1861]
Osbourn's Music Saloon, Philadelphia, PA
The Parish Choir [1888], Boston, MA
John Perry and Co. [1878]
J. Power's Music and Instrument Warehouse [1808], London
Preston and Son [1799], London
Root and Cady [1864], Chicago, IL
Jos. W. Stern [1902]
Henry Waterson, Inc. [1925]
Sep. Winner and Co. [1864], Philadelphia, PA

School Song Index

Some responses listed two or more alma maters and/or two or more fight songs. The first song in each category has been accepted as the school's official song for the purposes of this directory.

Above the Ohio (am), 137
ACC (am), 79
AC Fite!! (fs), 56
Across the Field (ofs), 98, 106
Across the Quad at Eventide (am), 129
Adeline, the Yale Boola Girl (o), 18
Adelphi University Fight Song (fs), 79
Adrian Alma Mater (am), 56
Against St. Lawrence Spirit (ofs), 85
Aggie Fight (fs), 13
Aggie's Fight (fs), 101
Aggies Fight Song (fs), 78
Ah, Well I Remember (am), 16
Alaska Pacific U (am), 4
Albion, Dear Albion (am), 56
Albright Fight Song (fs), 106
All Hail (am), 14
All Hail Arizona (o), 6
All Hail! Blue and Gold (am), 12
All Hail, CAC (am), 5
All Hail Green and Gold (am), 8
All Hail, Green and Gold (am), 8
All Hail Muskingum (am), 97
All Hail! O Davidson! (am), 89
All Hail to Austin Peay (am), 119
All Hail to Kazoo (fs), 58
All Hail to Thee, Dear NCC (am), 104
All Hail to Thee, Oh Waldorf (am), 39
All Hail to Washington State (ofs), 135

All Sons and Daughters (am), 81
All True Daughters of Our Lady (am), 98
Alma College Alma Mater (am), 56
Alma College Fight Song (fs), 56
Alma Mater (am)
  Adelphi University, 79
  Alabama State University, 1
  Alaska Methodist University, 4
  Albright College, 106
  Alice Lloyd College, 43
  Amherst College, 50
  Atlanta University, 22
  Atlantic Christian College, 88
  Bergen Community College, 75
  Bethany College, 135
  Bethel College, Indiana, 31
  Bethel College, Kansas, 40
  Bethel College, Minnesota, 61
  Bloomsburg University, 106
  Bluffton College, 95
  Boston University, 51
  California Baptist College, 8
  California Lutheran University, Thousand
    Oaks, 8
  California State University, Chico, 9
  California State University, Dominguez
    Hills, 9
  California State University, Hayward, 9
  California University of Pennsylvania, 107

196   SCHOOL SONG INDEX

ROBERT F. O'BRIEN is Director of Bands Emeritus at the University of Notre Dame. He has published his own musical compositions and numerous articles for music and industry publications.